Ignite Your Passion Kindle Your Internal Spark

April M. Williams Productions

1st Edition

Published in the United States of America

Published by April M. Williams and CyberLife Tutors

Algonquin, IL 60102

www.CyberLifeTutors.com

Electronic ISBN NOOK KINDLE, PDF 978-0-9841807-1-4

Print ISBN 978-0-9841807-4-5

Acknowledgements

Many people participated in creating this book including those of a certain age who find themselves at a crossroads looking for a map. Through discussions with generous people in a variety of fields, I was inspired to pave a new road for myself.

Mary Margaret Maule had faith in me from the first time we met and Lisa Deon inspired me with her passion for humorous storytelling.

Thanks to Lori Albert and Lou Camp for editorial input. Cover art by Kyle E. Williams with photograph by April M. Williams.

Alexis, Carson and Kyle thanks for sharing your unique sparks with me. My deepest gratitude to my husband and best friend Noel F. Williams who always has my back. He encourages me to explore and find my passions in life.

- AMW

Introduction

"I am just not interested in my work anymore."

"Work is just a job. I want to do something meaningful with my life."

"Is this all there is?"

Hearing comments like these is how this book began. I knew how they felt because I had experienced the same feelings. My work no longer excited me, the passion for my work was gone and our customers at the large corporation where I worked seemed distant. I did not feel like I was making a difference in their lives.

This book was ignited by the passion or more accurately, the lack of passion I felt in myself and saw in others. Over the past few years, I struggled with these same feelings before identifying an opportunity to connect with customers directly. It was important to me to see the results of my work and how my actions positively impacted others.

When I talk about passion, I mean the exhilarating feeling which comes over you when you are immersed in that which you love. You are excited to get started and content to stay engaged in your work. You feel fulfilled and complete in what you are doing. Some people seem to find their passion as early as their teen years while others of us take much longer to find that spark that ignites the fire inside of us.

In 2008 I founded CyberLife Tutors www.cyberlifetutors.com providing customers more business through social media marketing. It is a wonderful feeling to work directly with companies and see immediate results. The passion is back in my work.

How did my experiences lead to this book? As both my professional and personal life evolved, I pondered many questions. What is it that gets me out of bed in the morning? How do I become inspired and motivated to achieve my best at whatever I choose to do? Why are certain activities so much easier to start and stick to?

My professional career changed direction several times and continues to evolve. I am most fulfilled when my passion is my career and now it is also my business. This metamorphosis was not a simple overnight occurrence but a process which took several years to complete. Even now the journey continues. For me, it's a wonderful feeling to spend my days doing what I have a passion for. As I continue along my travels, I found others who are just as passionate about their work. They are easy to spot because their passion emanates from every pore in their body.

That is how this book began. As I talked to others who had a passion for their occupations, I asked them if they would be willing to share their stories with you. In this book, my co-authors contribute their personal experiences in transition and finding their passion in life. In their stories, you will see what they are passionate about, how they found their passion and how you can find your passion.

Best,

April M. Williams

President, CyberLife Tutors

Stop Falling Down in 3 Easy Steps: Turn Job Loss into Opportunity!

By Christopher McCann

Are you playing it safe but feeling trapped in the life you have created for yourself? How do you know when it's time to move on from a job, a relationship, or even the city you live in? Is the reason you don't reach your goals because you don't care anymore? You may not have a clear vision of where you want to go, but you may realize that you need to leave where you are.

Often times the best strategy to achieve victory in life's battles is to "burn the boats behind us." Times may be a bit lean right now but the truth is that this is a great opportunity to grow. Before you write me off as crazy, listen to what I have experienced regarding job loss, income issues, and any of life's major challenges.

1. If you lost your job, that's a wonderful thing because it's going to make you stronger. People will come to me and tell me they quit their job, lost it, or got laid off. Invariably my response is congratulations! That's awesome! I can say that because I know they are about to go through a monstrous growth experience. There are lots of people who lose their jobs and feel a sense of relief, as if some enormous burden has been lifted. It's all in your mind and how you react depends entirely on your perspective, how you react is under your control. You can see it as a huge opportunity, or not. Your goal shouldn't be to live a cozy, secure and safe life as-you'll have plenty of opportunity to do that when you're 6 feet under, in a nice little box. No one will bug you then.

2. Start thinking about what you really want to do. Maybe you're not strong enough to lift that weight yet, but you can start developing your courage and skills in that direction. What kinds of goals inspire you right now? Don't look at the easy ones, but the ones that will lift you up. Re-frame it from "Oh my God, holy !@#$ into "here we go, this is a gift, it'll make

me stronger". Now we need to get clear about what we really want and moving us towards that, what gets us fired up.

3. Ask yourself what kinds of goals inspire you right now. If you move towards your inspiration fully, learn from your passion, and share it ith the world, you can't fail! There's a balance between being freaked out and accepting the challenge. What's a simple way of finding the balance between challenge and being freaked out? Grow a pair! Helen Keller said life is a daring adventure or nothing. There is no in-between. The challenge is what makes you stronger. It's the equivalent of going to the gym and lifting the same weight day after day. What's the point? You're not going to get any stronger? How long are you going to stick with the 10 pound dumbbells? Progress! Get stronger! Of course it's harder to lift the heavy weights; you'd be bored and frustrated by a lack of growth. There's no need to fear it or resist it, even though it's called resistance training. Let the resistance come from life itself, not from what's within you.

When I first got into the habit of setting goals, people told me I should set S.M.A.R.T goals (specific, measurable, attainable, realistic and timely). It was very methodical but it didn't work well for me. It's not that I didn't want to achieve my S.M.A.R.T goals, but they never consistently got my butt in motion to do anything about them. What did work for me was scrapping that whole process by looking at the goals I had already accomplished and compared them to the goals that I hadn't. What I found was that the goals I achieved weren't usually the S.M.A.R.T ones (or those pushed on me by others). What set me in motion were the goals that inspired and drove me to action the minute I thought about them. When I set goals today, if it doesn't change the way I feel (my physiology or emotional state) immediately, then I know it's a bad goal. I won't bother with it any longer.

Not too long ago I made a decision to "burn the boats" with my career and begin, again. It used to annoy me to no end when people would suggest that the things you did as a child are what

you should do for a living. Am I supposed to collect baseball cards or build tree forts in my mid-30's? Seriously? Yet when I made that decision to peer down the rabbit hole, what struck me were the verbs I kept using. What I really enjoyed was coaching youth sports teams (even though I was a kid myself), organizing events and creating art. I would immerse myself so deeply in those projects that I'd lose track of time. I loved how it felt to help people, encourage that kid to make his first free throw, catch their first fish or actually hit a baseball. I loved seeing that "a-ha" moment in people's eyes from a very early age. How could I get back in touch with wanting to inspire people, have fun helping and connecting with them, give them back to themselves and still have a career? The more work I've done towards that in my own career, the more the goals themselves have inspired me. The funny thing is that somewhere along the line I began to achieve it; it inspired me, drove me to action and created a specific result. I am no longer adopting socially conditioned goals, where I set them, start working on them then realize deep down I just don't give a damn. My S.M.A.R.T. goals were about what other people wanted, not what inspired me.

I realized that I needed to start setting inspiring goals. One of the questions I asked myself was; how do I tease out that motivation regarding what I wanted in life? One of the first steps I learned was disconnecting what I don't want. You may find yourself in a trap where your life is filled with things you don't want or don't feel connected to. They leave you feeling uninspired. Maybe you're in a city you don't want to live in, or a job you don't like or a relationship where you feel stuck. Granted, it's counter-intuitive to shed what you don't want in order to create space for what you do want (at this point you may be asking yourself "Who is this guy and is he serious? It's a crappy job market and I'm going to leave what I do have, behind? It's better than nothing!") As Steven Covey <https://www.stephencovey.com/7habits/7habits-habit4.php> says, go for win-win or no deal. Too many of us think that compromise is the best solution. Personally, I'd rather be homeless than be in a situation that's uninspiring. Did I burn the boats? Absolutely. You have to burn the ships that got you there when you land on the new shore. However, you don't want to burn the food and supplies! I'm guilty of this and have learned the hard way a few times. Make a careful distinction between what you need (food and supplies) vs. the escape route that's keeping you tied to that ship. It's no different than going through a divorce, you've got to leave, but damn you wish you had grabbed that end table. It's possible to balance passion and practicality.

After burning the ships, you've taken it far enough to where you are committed. If you have to quit your job to move forward (and a lot of people do) the job isn't only the food and supplies, it's the ship as well! That's what may very well be keeping us in the wrong harbors. In our parents and grandparents generation, the idea was that you picked a job and did that for life. We've inherited the ability to not question our circumstances or choices we made years ago. It's not that I woke up one morning and turned the corner; it was a gradual malaise, a long slow curve, which developed over time. It took me years to realize what was happening to me no matter how many times I had heard it from others. I couldn't mute my feelings any longer, and made the conscious decision to recreate myself. There's a part of me that wants to shake the hell out of the people I interact with, rip the heart out of my chest and stick it in theirs! By heart I mean courage. The definition of courage is "the state or quality of mind or spirit that enables one to face danger, fear, or vicissitudes with self-possession, confidence, and resolution; bravery." The word courage is derived from the Latin cor "to say it with all the heart; to be sincere." Ask yourself; does this path I'm on have a heart?

You'll know it has heart because you can feel it in your chest. It excites you and you have an emotional reaction to it. At the same time it can scare the hell out of you and give you the feeling of "wow, that would be awesome but I don't know if I can pull it off." These are the goals that should really inspire you! Excitement is part inspiration and part terror. I have to be somewhat scared about the path I'm on because that's the path that is building my "core". It's scary out there and so many of us are playing it safe! Find that edge, that thing you feel in your chest that both scares and excites you. Safe is an adjective and a noun, it means both free from harm and an enclosed locked container. If you're living the noun you're living the adjective as well. The need for security is restricting your freedom. If the basis of your self esteem is your need for security, a safe relationship or a steady paycheck, you're living in a cage.

What does it look like to take a step outside of that? Initially it's terrifying! At the same time it's thrilling. From a pretty early age, I made a conscious decision to create difficulty in my life as a means of creating growth. It's been long, progressive training, no different than using dumbbells to strength train. For someone who has been stuck, changing jobs is a huge weight to lift. It's like a "newbie" looking at a 100-pound dumbbell, thinking that's too much weight to curl. Yet everyone is at a different level of courage, only able to tolerate a level of uncertainty. You need to have a vision of where you are going when it comes to the application of courage. Ask yourself "where do I want to be? What shore am I sailing to" then burn the ship! How important is that vision of where you want to be? It depends if you're in more of a training or destination mindset. There are times when I have goals that are just about training. Maybe there is something I'm afraid of where I need to build my courage, a fear I need to get over, then I'll go do it. Maybe after that, the vision is more about competition so it's more performance mode than practice. Performance mode is applying the strength I've already built. As any athlete knows, there's a big difference between practice and games. If all they did were play games, they wouldn't be great athletes because practice puts you in as many potential scenarios as possible.

Do you find yourself worried about your job and the possibility of losing it? Wondering what to do if you've already lost your job? How can you turn that job loss into a positive opportunity? How can focusing on your passion, rather than paying your bills actually help build a more satisfying life? We all have been at the "oh !@#$, what am I gonna do" part. Some of us will look at the glass being half empty and some half full. This path I'm sharing with you of courage and inspiration seems like the high, unrealistic and impractical road. There is a hidden benefit to losing your job. It is going to make you stronger. It's very true that whatever doesn't kill you will make you stronger. You may be running deeper and deeper into debt, even on the verge of bankruptcy. You know what? You will still be here. Your life won't end; it'll only make you stronger and wiser. You'll have plenty of time to relax when you're six feet under. You will have built skills that may have never developed if you hadn't gone through that experience.

When people lose their jobs, they really start thinking hard about their lives, maybe for the first time in quite awhile. You may be feeling a mixture of panic and relief. Almost always they're losing a job they didn't really want (which is often the reason why they lost it). They were expendable. They were fired or laid off because they weren't really needed. They weren't doing work that they were passionate about. It's not very common that people who are passionate are fired or laid off. They are usually awesome to be around and management is going to let that person go last and only if they absolutely have to. That person is probably doing more work than anyone else and they're creating a ton of value. Knowing those things to be true, turn inward, determine what you're really passionate about, what you'd really like to do and how can you create that.

Don't focus too much on the "how" right away...it's the why. Ask yourself, what would that kind of life be like, and start feeling that passion once again. That passion and excitement is what's going to get you into action! Job security is finding that passion, adding energy, and contributing. That's what people want to be around. You are adding energy; you're a contributor. A manager of 10 employees that has to layoff two is NOT going to lay off those that have the energy, passion and contribute. They're going to lay off those that are miserable, unproductive, that don't really fit, those that aren't easy get along with and that don't want to be there. The manager is actually doing them a favor by laying them off! Those are the individuals that really DO need that wakeup call! If I've been laid off, and I'm sitting here reading this trying to shift my perspective, there is incentive for me to dig deep and find out what I'm inspired by because that's going to make me more attractive. Take the time and find out what fires you up because THAT is going to make you more marketable and relevant. Inspiration is absolutely critical. I've worked for a time without it and a great deal of time with it. After experiencing both sides of that fence I could never go back to working without it.

When you're passionate, filled with energy, happy and contributing, you find yourself inspiring people in ways that you can't even imagine!

When I truly became successful in this business, it wasn't when I started consistently making six figures; it was when I made the decision to start helping and inspiring people. People say do what you love and the money will follow. I find that it's somewhat accurate, but you have to understand why that is the case. When you do what you love, you do it often and you get good at it. If you keep working at it, for 10,000 hours (according to Outliers) you're going to become great! I imagine this is only true if you work at it intelligently and passionately, rather than making the same mistakes over and over. Eventually you'll create some value for other people. Now you have some talent that you can share, use and teach other people how to do what you're doing. Then you can create income by exchanging value with others. It started for me with awareness of finding my passion, really focusing on it, developing it and sharing it with others.

Just because you made your bed doesn't mean you have to lie in it. I no longer believe that I have to live with my past decisions, choices, and actions. Thank God. The past is past and has nothing to do with me. It has nothing to do with now. Do not let anything from your past inhibit you as you go about re-creating yourself. At some point we have to determine if it's a higher priority to abandon our soul, ourselves... or to actually have the life we want.

About the author:

Christopher McCann is always looking for ways to maintain, enhance and develop our culture while keeping the core values we had from day one. From the beginning we were a flat and collaborative organization with a lack of hierarchy. We want all of our employees to be involved in growing and developing our uniqueness. It may be coming up with different programs or processes or just being there to talk with people. It's an incredible tribe of people and I love "pollinating" in the morning knowing that in some way, I've made a difference in their lives.

Igniting Your Passion

Gaye Mack

Even though it was over 40 years ago, I recall one of my college professors in Comparative Religions making the following statement; *"Whatever it is that you are most passionate about, regardless of subject, this is your religion."* Inexplicably, those words have stuck with me all these years, most likely because he wasn't talking about 'religion' in the traditional sense but because he was talking about things that make your soul sing...your passion.

Since that time, I've been fortunate to discover many (sometimes too many!) passions that make my soul sing. The journey hasn't been easy; it's not meant to be easy. Some of these passions remain, others have outlived their usefulness or I have outlived them. Some of them, when yanked from my life regardless of circumstances, have left me bereft with the feeling that nothing would ever fill the hole. And yet, some have appeared through a doorway nothing short of astonishing, which is how my passion for writing came full blown into my life, although along a very circuitous route.

You could say I began writing when I was fifteen. Almost every young girl writes when she's fifteen, usually in a journal, which was called a 'diary' in my day. While I liked to write, it wasn't a 'passion' then. Years later college came along, but passionate isn't quite how I would describe the energy behind producing endless term papers. Then after I was married in my mid-twenties, something happened. I suddenly started dreaming about writing a book. On long car rides I'd get lost in my thoughts (thankfully my husband was driving!) and he'd ask me, "What are you thinking about?" I'd reply, "I'm writing my book" and that's where my book stayed; in my mind.

Fast forward twenty years. In the midst of my forties I landed what I thought was the 'dream corporate job' of my life. But, strangely, as time marched on I slowly became restless and over-the-top stressed. Four years down the road, I couldn't make myself resign. I was always thinking 'it will get better.' Truth is, I wasn't listening to my intuition. I wasn't paying attention to the subtle messages that were right in front of me to pick up the pen (metaphorically speaking) and write. As a result I was given a louder message; I was in the wrong spot, wrong career…my health spiraled downward and it was a hard lesson.

A key to finding your passion is to listen to your gut, your intuition. Each of us possesses 'innate wisdom' that continually whispers messages to us, trying to keep us zeroed in on our Soul's lifetime agenda so that we may manifest our greatest good. However, we, all of us, possess an ego and the ego loves to be in charge. It likes to distract us from the deeper influence of this wisdom which makes it difficult, if not impossible, to hear these messages clearly. Ego fights surrendering our Mental Plan to our Soul's Plan and as we continue in our resistance a forewarning typically appears in our lives. This alerts us to the fact that we must shift our emotional perspective. Unheeded, these Soul-messages can manifest in difficult life-events and/or relationships and the dominos begin to fall. Our emotions start to reel unpleasantly out of balance, and then, as it was in my case, it's only a matter of time before the body ceases to function in a harmonious way.

When we ignore our intuition, our Soul messages, we teeter on the edge of our abyss, not just once, but repeatedly. Fear and despair are reflected in the belief that we don't have operating instructions, maps or tools to manage the next right step. This belief, fueled by our ego acting as the Trickster and Crazy-maker, creates havoc that becomes anchored in our emotional body. In our fears and terrors the ego tells us we're headed for disaster if we risk taking the leap of faith to act on the passion held in our dreams.

Because I teetered on the edge of my own abyss, I entered what seemed an endless period of declining health. Then I lost my 'dream job' due to the global political situation at the time. I look back now and marvel at how resistant I was, how powerfully my fear to make changes prevented me from 'following my passion.'

Finally, after seeing numerous specialists, enduring a myriad of inconclusive tests, a friend suggested I seek out an evaluation by a western-trained physician who practiced classical homeopathy and Ayurvedic medicine. While theoretically I subscribed to the philosophy of these systems of medicine, for me to actually *participate* was another matter all together. Nevertheless, my desperation pushed me off the cliff; I took my first leap of faith, my first course correction in changing what wasn't working. Little did I suspect that this leap would evolve into manifesting my long ignored passion.

This jump not only put me on the path to recovering my health but it catapulted me headlong into the healing field of mind/body/spirit medicine and the work of British physician Dr. Edward Bach. Famous for pioneering the now famous 38 Bach flower remedies in the late 1920's, Bach died at the early age of 50 in 1936. However his work has lived on at a global level that he couldn't have possibly foreseen as it's undeniably recognized as one of the foremost therapies in mind/body/spirit medicine.

Considered vibrational medicine and homeopathic in nature, the energy of flower remedies assists us by supporting and shifting our perspectives that have become skewed when we are emotionally distressed. The emotions involved can be those that commonly come and go as a result of daily life to those more complex feelings that are held deeply within us, entrenched in our emotional history. The remedies are capable of awakening us to our Soul's intention and action. This is at their core; this is what Bach knew.

When I was first introduced to these remedies as part of my own healing process, something 'clicked.' I *knew* this work was the next step down the road of my course correction. Here at last was my new passion, intriguing me so much that I wanted to know more, I wanted to work with them as a practitioner. The question was, how would this be possible? The Bach Centre was, and still is, located outside of Oxford, England. At first, because I have extended family in Oxford, I thought if I could just get there the Bach Center (and my 'family') would welcome me with open arms... a delusion on my part. When I contacted the Centre asking for information on education to become a practitioner, I was politely but firmly told that (a) they were backlogged nine months and besides (b) their courses were only open to British practitioners. I was devastated. Then, surprisingly, almost a year later a door opened.

I was working part time in the holistic medical practice I'd first sought out regarding my own health. Unexpectedly a card came in the mail to the office from the Bach Center announcing the new practitioner educational program in the US...one of the cities on the list was Chicago! Going forward, I spent the next three years in attaining the status as one of the first Bach Foundation Registered Practitioners in the United States. To imply this process was easy would be misleading. Initially, I had no money for the courses, but little by little ways for me to participate did show up, often through my shameless begging to volunteer during the weekend courses in exchange for tuition reduction.

More doors opened. I began a small private practice by seeing people most of whom were already participating in some form of traditional psychotherapy. At the same time I went to graduate school while also working as a U.S. educational 'retail' trainer for the Bach Foundation. My work grew. I found myself giving private workshops around the US and in Britain along with 'one-off' speaking engagements to groups and at international conferences. This led to...at last, writing by contributing articles for various publications. However, despite all of this activity, I *still* wasn't writing like I *felt* I wanted to; something was missing.

Then, unpredictably, I was asked by a British publisher in the field of mind/body/spirit philosophy, to write a book on the spiritual aspects of Dr. Bach and his work. Once I started working on the book, I was off and running; this was the first glimmer of what I'd been waiting for. Nevertheless, like everything before it, the journey was a long one of learning to navigate the foreign landscape of creating a book, working with a wonderful editor who dropped into my life as a gift (and still is!) seeing it published, experiencing first-hand the harsh reality of what this writing work takes. This was not a cakewalk by any stretch of the imagination, but it didn't matter. I was locked into my long dreamt passion to produce more substantial writing.

Igniting Soul Fire, Spiritual Dimensions of the Bach Flower Remedies was released in the UK and US in 2005 and later translated into German. My next book, *Making Complementary Therapies Work for You* was released in 2006. This was followed by *The View, Mind over Matter, Heart over Mind-From Conan Doyle to 'Conversations with God'* released in 2009. I'm honored to be a contributing author for *The View* along with Neale Donald Walsch, Ervin Laszlo, Peter Russell and other notable contributors.

After I finished writing my contribution for The View, I took a break from writing (but not my Bach work) as I'd been drawn (or so I thought) to a different interest. I entered into a partnership with a good friend to work with groups of women. But at the end of four years, while we had been successful, I knew this just wasn't *my* work. We agreeably dissolved the partnership and I went back to writing. This time I returned to historical fiction, which I'd dabbled with in the early 90's.

To recount the journey this aspect of my writing has so far taken me down the road less traveled would take another chapter! Without question, because of the current publishing landscape, it has brought home a comment made to me by an author in the early 1970's when I told her I wanted to write a fiction book. She said, *"This will be the loneliest, hardest, work you will ever do."* However, passions ignore such advice; passions ignore most scrooge-type advice.

Because the drive behind them is so intense, they will not be ignored. This is why I have poet Marge Piercy's quote over my desk to look at when all seems lost, when more disappointment than I think I can stand overwhelms me. Passion is about perseverance. Marge reminds me that *"The real writer is one who really writes. Talent is an invention like phlogiston after the fact of fire. Work is its own cure. You have to like it better than being loved."*

While she's referring to the craft of writing, her words easily apply to whatever you find your passion to be. In your own pursuit you must be dogged; it isn't easy. Even if you are uncertain what your passion might be, you can be sure there are clues whispering to you in some way. It's a matter of being awake, paying attention and listening. In order to do this you must be:

Quiet.

You must ask yourself, all things being equal, what is it you truly want and why?

You must ask, what is it that you can provide that is special? You may not find the cure for Cancer, but we never can know how we have positively affected someone else's life by (in our mind) the smallest thing.

And, most importantly, you must ask yourself who you are and who you want to be?

You just might be surprised.

About the author:

Throughout her life Gaye has held a deep interest in esoteric philosophies, spirituality in medicine, international travel and writing. Currently she's working on a 12th century mystery series set in Great Britain and studying evolutionary astrology under Steven Forrest. She keeps her linen closet and family in the Chicago area.

http://www.gayemack.com/blog

http://www.facebook.com/gayemackauthor

http://www.amazon.com/-/e/B0034PPLWU

http://www.gayemack.com

The Object of My Addiction

By Lisa Deon

I have, for as long as I can recall, loved horses. Like many young girls I craved the freedom they represented, the bonding between horse and rider, and their all around natural grace and beauty. With zeal I daydreamed about being able to leap upon the back of a noble steed, flying like the wind in whatever direction we chose. Of course, reality is so much different than fantasy.

We lived in the suburbs and no matter how much I cajoled and pleaded, my parents could not reconcile themselves to keeping a horse in our tiny back yard. So I settled for the next available thing; absorbing the horse through books by Marguerite Henry and Walter Farley. In my mind I was marooned with The Black Stallion. I lived on Chincoteague Island with the hardy little ponies. In Victorian England I felt the cruel lash of a whip while pulling a Hansom Cab over cobblestone streets as Black Jack, the carriage horse. I collected Breyer models and Sam Savitt posters. I adorned my room with Arabs, Morgans and even that ugly old grey milk cart model that wore a straw hat. I never walked anywhere, I trotted, or if in a hurry, I galloped, making snorting noises and pawing at the ground with my sneaker covered hooves. I attached a jump rope to the handlebars of my bike and taught myself, not always successfully, to ride using "reins". Each waking breath was devoted to thinking of, reading of and dreaming of horses.

As I got older and became a popular sitter for the neighborhood children, at fifty cents an hour, I saved up my earnings and enrolled in riding lessons through the local park district. I was in heaven as I shuttled to and from the stable in the district's van every Thursday evening. Learning to ride was empowering; the feeling of all that muscle under you, controlled by your commands, a delicate dance of balance and forward impulsion. The knowledge that such an enormous animal is responding to cues given by you builds courage, confidence and self esteem. It made me realize that as I controlled the animal I could also control my life.

At 13 I attended a company picnic with my family and found, to my delight, pony rides. By then I was too old and equitationally advanced to do something so infantile, but the man who ran the business offered me a job working for him. At the princely sum of $1.00 an hour, I jumped at the opportunity.

My goal was never to be at the pinnacle of the horsemanship world. I only knew that I wanted to be involved with them. The details never mattered; boarding, training, riding, driving, as long as I had contact and was able to inhale their intoxicating warm scent, combined with the smell of sweat and leather. The exultation I felt while watching their powerful muscles ripple under sleek fur groomed to perfection. I enjoyed learning the difference in their vocalizations: the "I'm hungry" whinny so different from the "It's scary" snorty inhale, so far removed from the "Where is everybody?" call.

Although it was a rewarding job because of my proximity to the ponies, it became clear that ponies are not like horses, at least the ones in this little string. They were sneaky, conniving little buggers who would just as soon stomp on your foot as look at you. I quit that job, not because of the rotten little Shetlands, but because the owner reneged on his $1 an hour and changed it to $5 a day.

Obsessed or not, I knew the value of my time.

Eventually, life overrode my horse habit, the constant "Oh grow up. Having horses is a little girl's dream," grinding into my psyche. I settled into being a passive observer, going on the occasional trail ride or watching the Thoroughbreds race at the track.

Eventually I married a man who was a closet cowboy, born in the wrong time and geographic location, who shared my love for horses. We took riding lessons together, ironically offered through the park district, and often discussed how we would both like to own a horse someday.

It was during this time in my life that I had an epiphany; my husband and I were in the car, driving past a field in Wisconsin. I could see across the light brown wheat to the edge of the plowed land. There were riders on horseback, trotting together in a group, kicking up dust. A small tribe out for an evening ride. The sun was setting; the rays filtering through the atmosphere giving everything it touched an ethereal quality. Filmmakers and photographers call this "the golden hour", and I knew that, where those people were, riding their horses through that field, in the company of one another, with the companionship of their horses; I knew that was where I wanted to be. That was where I had always wanted to be, but somehow I had allowed myself to be sidetracked. My envy was palatable. I had become a victim of the dream smashers, the "Be practical" shouters. I had become a hostage of the reason-pirates; the connivers who conspire to steal your heart's desire and replace it with a 9-5 job, expecting that in the frenzy of daily living you'll never notice the difference.

With double income and no kids, my husband and I settled into our jobs and a house of our own. One June evening after a particularly enjoyable lesson, we looked at each other and one of us said, "I think 'someday' has come."

We shopped around, and eventually purchased an Appaloosa, L.P. Prairie Dreamer and began our new life as horse owners. Once again I became absorbed into the culture of horses. The riding, grooming, equipment and vocabulary were my drug of choice, an addiction I threw my entire soul into. I had finally come home, and reveled in the feeling of satisfaction, in knowing that after my daily grind at the 9 to 5'er, I could once again drive out to the stable and get my horse fix.

A year after the purchase, we had a daughter. Now the stable became my escape, my "me" time. After work my husband would return home and care for our child and I would race to the barn, allowing myself the luxury of relaxing with my equine obsessed friends. Not long after that my husband was offered a job transfer to Missouri. Although not born in Illinois, I always considered myself a native, and the move to Missouri would take me far from friends and family. I agreed to go, on one condition: I wanted horse property. Not content with keeping my best non-human friend at a stable, I wanted to be able to look out my kitchen window and watch him grazing contently.

Of course after we moved, horse mathematics came into play; three people and one horse equals two people who are horseless, so we purchased a large pony that could be ridden by adults as well as the daughter who I knew would be genetically horse-obsessed. And of course if you own a mare, you are required to breed her. Then when another pony was offered for free we had to take her in too...

It was then I realized that besides merely loving horses, I was passionate about them. I started reading about horses again, this time not novels but non-fiction. I wanted to absorb everything I could about them; learn how horses thought, how they moved, how breed form followed function. I immersed myself in my Appaloosa's pedigree, trying to figure out how his genetics factored into his development as a saddle horse. As she grew, our daughter got into 4-H, and I learned even more, absorbing all the Hippology workbooks and information they presented to the children at the meetings.

Eventually our time on the farm in Missouri came to a close and we moved even further west, landing in Utah. We chose a home in the suburbs, victims of the huge difference in real estate prices, and soured on the work involved in maintaining a hobby farm. Only able to afford board for one horse, we found homes for the others and brought Dreamer along. And so I still had him, my first horse, that animal I had craved to know for so long.

After less than a year in Salt Lake I was hired as a carriage driver. The job involved maneuvering the big draft horses through the streets downtown, giving romantic rides and historic tours. Once again I was a student, learning the art of driving, the harness tack and the finesse necessary to negotiate in traffic; understanding what the horses see as a danger and what they ignore. I enjoyed teaching passersby, some of whom have never encountered a real horse in their lives, what this magnificent animal with such a noble past is capable of doing. It is a job I still hold today, and I always tell people that it is the best, the most fun, intriguing and rewarding job I have ever had, something which few people can honestly say about their professions.

Several years ago I finally found a way to balance my passion for horses with another love. Having always been a voracious reader, I became a writer, blogging about my carriage driving life, along with creating fictional characters and scenes. I've found through the years my horse experience has transferred over into my writing, and that's my genre — writing about characters that live and work with horses on a daily basis. I hope that I, too, as those wonderful novelists before me, may someday fan that spark in a person who loves horses as much as I have. Encourage them to take that passion and turn it into something they can do for a living, whether is as a breeder, trainer, writer, or a person who gives pony rides.

Combine that obsession which burns within you, and turn it into something you can incorporate into the rest of your life.

About the author:

Lisa Deon <Lisa@LisaDeon.com> used to share her tales by cornering people at cocktail parties and telling them stories until someone had to give up and go pee. Finally, she thought to write them down. Her favorite foods are wine and popcorn and her favorite smell is horse. Connect with Lisa at her website www.LisaDeon.com, or Amazon.com <http://amzn.to/YrSqd9>. "The Carriage Trade" available at Amazon, Smashwords, and Createspace. "Splitting the Difference" available exclusively for Kindle from Amazon.

Falling Into Passion

Tara Bider

I always felt terrible when I was a kid and someone would ask me what I wanted to be when I grew up and I had no answer. Even through college, I wasn't sure I was committed to any one major and nothing struck me as a career in any form. Did I like people? I guess. Was I good with numbers? Kind of. What about Science? Nope. But the other kids who professed loudly in kindergarten that they wanted to be a teacher or a doctor grew up to be just those things.

As a freshman in college, my roommate wanted to be a Reproductive Endocrinologist. Really? I didn't even know what that was until I had my own fertility problems at age 30. Guessing that this early sense of knowing what you wanted in life stemmed from parental influence, I often wondered if I'd grow to follow in my parents' footsteps. Daughter of a farmer-turned secretary-turned HR Manager? Or a mid-level Data Processing Supervisor? Neither seemed like a spectacular career path to me, although completely respectable.

My brother had an early interest in planes. I had no early interests. My sister was talented in Art. I am not creative in the least. For a number of years I remember my standard line became telling people that I wasn't good at any ONE thing, but pretty good at a LOT of things. Several times throughout my graduate school internship I heard people remark that Social Workers become Social Workers "for a reason". I always snickered silently when I heard that because my own journey into Social Work was not all that profound.

I'd ended up in Social Work via the following avenue: started as a freshman in a liberal arts college as an International Business major, with a minor in Swedish. I transferred to a state university between semesters as a sophomore into the School of Social Work because there were only two schools within the university that accepted mid-year entries: Social Work or Aircraft Maintenance. A no-brainer, since I had no aviation training whatsoever. A social worker by default? It hardly seemed like the significant and noble reason people end up in that profession.

But I did find that I was interested in the subject matter and enjoyed sociologic research. The more time I spent learning about Social Work, the more interested I became. The better I did in school, the better my college experience was altogether. The more effort I put into it, the more I sought to excel in that career. But there was still a desire gap. Other classmates wanted to be School Social Workers! And Mental Health counselors! And advocates for abused children!

And me? I just wanted to finish grad school and have some letters behind my name. For several years after graduation, I enjoyed working in the medical field as part of an interdisciplinary team that cared for trauma patients. Being a hospital social worker wasn't "my passion" per se—but I liked the fact that I was surrounded by very intelligent and skilled people in an exciting environment.

Still, there was always an undeniable undercurrent in my professional life and I constantly felt like I was wandering. Would I ever mature and finally know exactly what I wanted out of life?

During lunch at the hospital one day, someone introduced me to a book about a mountaineering accident on Mt. Everest. "You'll love it!!" they sang. I resisted. "You won't be able to put it down!" I shrugged. "These people get 'summit fever'; you just HAVE to read it!" I stared blankly and asked, "What is 'summit fever'?" We live in the Midwest where there are no mountains, why would I possibly read a book about climbing Mt. Everest?

I don't know exactly what prompted me to finally read the book, but I did. I was shocked at the tale. And curious. And saddened. And fascinated. I also wondered where I had been in life so as not to have heard about the disaster when it actually took place. Did I live under a rock? How had I not heard of something of that magnitude? Why? Because I didn't care about the mountains. I had no attachment to them.

I think of all the things ever printed about that accident, to this day I have probably read 99% of them. I have read and viewed the personal accounts of the tragedy from all of the expeditions involved and the entire media onslaught that followed in the next decade.

The booked grabbed a hold of me immediately--so much that I brazenly signed up for an Introduction to Mountaineering course as soon as I finished the last page of that book's epilogue. This mountaineering course affirmed my lust for being in the mountains in general. It ignited a spark which catapulted me into pursuing a trip to Mt. Everest Base Camp. From there, I told myself, I would decide if I truly am drawn to this mountain and want to venture further towards her summit.

What was set in motion by reading one book is hard to explain. The more I knew about Mt. Everest, the more I wanted to know. I'm captivated when I see photographs of the Himalayas, when I read about Nepal, when I look at pictures of Sherpas and pujas and crampons and crevasses.

I lay out maps on my living room floor and try to get a sense of the grandeur of Asia's mountains. I research the pros and cons of approaching the mountain from the North in Tibet vs. the Southeast Ridge Route in Nepal. I argue with friends over whether climbing with supplemental oxygen negates the validity of summiting. I purchase various types of carabiners and read about knot making and study different types of climbing rope.

I memorize the top five highest mountains and their altitudes and recite them to my children on the way to pre-school. I sprinkle the phrase, "Someday when I go to Everest..." liberally in conversations.

This fascination fascinates me in and of itself. Is it because it is something so foreign from the way I currently live? I feel like I know so much about climbing Mt. Everest without actually having much high altitude experience. It borders on addiction some days.

For years I poured over catalogs, itineraries and gear lists from outfitters. I compared photos and journals from expeditions and trekking groups who've made the pilgrimage in the last 20 years. I've calculated and re-calculated the costs of tackling this dream, sometimes derailed by unexpected household repairs, insurance co-pays and expanding grocery bills but usually still managing to squirrel away $20 here, $50 there into my "Everest account". The pain of watching it build so slowly!

When my children were born, it was a whole new series of questions to ponder. Would I even be able to leave them for an extended period of time to visit this mountain?

My interest in Everest went through a new chapter of change while I was pregnant. After years of fertility treatments, including months of bed rest and hospitalizations (which allowed for huge amounts of reflection and introspection), an unexpected lung surgery surrounding my first pregnancy also put a new spin on my desire to see Everest. Every twitch, wheeze, pain, cough and subsequent lung collapse set off a fear that I would never realize my goal. After all, good lungs are essential at high altitude.

My fertility doctors and thoracic surgeon had a great impact on my mental discipline through all of those years of emotional and physical hardship, right up through In Vitro Fertilization procedures and a thoracotomy. Unbeknownst to me at the time, the constant patience, fortitude, resilience and courage I would need to get through my medical problems would turn out to serve me well as I climbed to 18,000 feet.

I learned to endure lots of pain during those treatment years and also learned to temper my disappointments and keep my emotions from reaching the extreme sides of the spectrum. I was constantly reminded that when the highs are high, the lows are in turn, very, very low. Just keep an even keel, I was repeatedly told. And I think that has been very good advice.

I have wanted Everest more than anything else I have ever wanted in my life, an especially huge feat in that I am fickle to the core about most things. And yet when someone remarks about my "passion" for Everest, it just doesn't seem like the word fits. I can't quite shake the notion that Everest is not my passion like everyone says. It's a very strong interest, sure. A desire coupled with a sense that I belong there, but it wasn't an innate desire. But who decides the definition of Passion? Are you born with it or is it something you discover one day by chance and it unfolds and snowballs over time? Is it merely because I happened upon this book that was pleasing to my senses and I became thirsty to know more?

The discovery of Passion may depend on the person. For me personally, I have taken Passion to mean that you have always wanted something particular, from your earliest memory, and you pursue it relentlessly. Have I always wanted Everest? The answer is no.

When I dissect it, I believe my own so-called Passion is my curiosity, which is energized by my open-minded spirit and willingness to alter my life's course. I don't know for sure, but it seems that Passion is also guided via the effort we put forth and the response we get back from the world around us. I can't say with 100% certainty that I am passionate about anything, but I do have a lot of things that intrigue me and am inexplicably drawn to, and undoubtedly Mt. Everest is one of those things.

Having finally realized my dream to trek to Everest Base Camp last year, it didn't satisfy my cravings but instead peeled back another layer of things I want to know about her. As I get older, my curiosity grows but I'm still cautious about placing labels on my desires. I have made peace, however, with the belief that opening your mind to the possibilities of the paths you will accidentally travel in your life is an important and meaningful beginning to finding your Passion.

About the author:

Tara Bider (jbider4252@aol.com) is a Licensed Clinical Social worker and mother to two smiley and energetic little boys. She is married to the most laid-back husband in the world, who indulges and accepts without question her unconventional ideas such as climbing Mt. Everest.

Tara's Everest blog can be found at http://suburban-sherpa.blogspot.com

Passion Ignited by a Simple Comment

By Peter Gault

A Little History: 1966. I was born at a very young age, (I think most of us probably have that in common). I grew up in Missouri – Independence and Kansas City. My mother is an immigrant from England, my father an Oklahoma born descendent of Welsh immigrants. Is it any wonder I'm a lover of British humor? My internal monologue sounds a lot like conversations between John Cleese, Billy Connolly, Eddie Izzard and Mike Myers as Austin Powers. Sometimes it gets a little crowded in there...

Fast forward..., 1985. I graduated from High School in Independence, Mo. I enjoyed a very short incomplete college career. At the time I was preoccupied with the events of life; family things that weren't going quite as planned.

Fast forward..., 1993. I was working as a medical insurance policy underwriter when I met my wife and best friend, over the phone. She was in Illinois. After somehow convincing her to come and see me in Kansas City, she moved there. Our first son was born, she moved back to Illinois. Fortunately I was invited along for the ride. That was October of 1993.

Fast forward..., 2010. That was almost 17 years ago. My wife and I have been together almost 18 years. Our kids, 2 boys 16 ½ and 14, and 1 girl, 11, are growing so quickly. Each of them enables me to create who I am.

I often forget to shell out the next bit of info at networking events, business mixers, which isn't very self serving. It's just not in my nature to define myself by what I do. So, before I forget...

What I do: I am so fortunate. I get to do what I love, what my passion is... Through the creative process of writing I get to help others tell their stories! My profession is Ghost Writing. I compose the words needed to help others tell their story and sell their products and services.

What I used to do: Human Resources, Business Development and management within the temporary staffing industry. For more than a decade my career focused on high level leadership, operational management, sales/marketing management and business development for the staffing industry. It was fun, allowed me the interaction with people that I so much enjoy and gave me the opportunity to be creative in business development projects.

Before I fell ass-backward into HR in the early 90's and subsequently Staffing, I did a LOT of things. Call Center Operations Management, Sales/Marketing Director, Customer Service Agent, Insurance Underwriting Agent (there's the writing word again) … Writing was always a part of every job I ever had and I always found a way to funnel in its creative process. Go figure.

April M. Williams, whom is bringing you this book, has tagged me as a passionate person and challenged me with an invitation to share the story of how I found my passion. It should be simple enough. Right? Yeah, right…

I've always allowed my inner voice to tell me that I enjoy being creative. As far back as I can remember I loved creative writing. I was one of those kids that almost always had a crayon, pencil, pen, something to write/draw/mark with in hand.

I can remember my mother teaching me to write my name before I started kindergarten. I learned the letters; P, E, T, E, R, G, A, U, L, T. I found more pleasure and fun in writing them in every order I could figure out. To me, the letters were my name and since it was my name I thought I should be able to write it in any way I chose. My mother, on the other hand, was completely frustrated.

I quickly learned to write out my name the way she wanted to see it. Then, I'd take a piece of paper and write the letters in any way I saw fit. To me, the letters of my name were simply pieces of a mosaic to be tossed in the air and let fall where they may.

My creative outlets grew through my childhood. My parents bought a broken player piano when I was 6. It was decided that since my dad couldn't repair the player mechanism, I would learn to play it for them. Thus music was ushered in. From childhood to young adulthood piano's, trumpets, baritones, drums, violins, violas, harmonicas all wandered in and out of my life. They were all fun but none of the instruments were a pleasure or passion in and of themselves.

In my adulthood painting, glass etching and wood carving introduced themselves. Again, all I enjoy but writing… Writing is something I always found time for, always did and still do. I simply love it.

I love words. Words have power, grace, beauty, horror and violence. My wife used to make fun of, but came to accept that, one of my favorite pass times was reading dictionaries and thesauruses. They're not all the same you know.

As I mentioned in my bio, I always found a way to incorporate the creative writing process in nearly every job I ever had. From policy and manual writing to sales and marketing writing. Often, even as a medical insurance underwriter, I'd volunteer for departmental procedural writing projects that other people dreaded. To me it was a blast. I was creating a tool that others would refer to, helping them do their jobs. I was creating something useful!

I did the same during the past decade + in my HR/Staffing career. I loved finding creative ways to develop business. Writing sales and marketing plans, copy and then implementing what I'd created was one of my most favorite things to do. I was quite happy in that career. And then there's that thing called change.

I had a cognitive discovery moment. That discovery enabled me to move past the 'I enjoy it' mentality to the 'I must do this!'

mentality. The moment was on Wednesday, August 5th 2009 shortly after 10am.

I was at a networking group. As a matter of fact, it's where I met April M. Williams. The meeting had ended; people were milling their way out. One of the group members commented on the monthly e-newsletter I wrote and produced for my employer at the time (there's that creative writing process I snuck in again).

He liked the newsletter and made a comment, something like; "You know I have clients that would pay good money to have people produce something like that for them." In a flash an idea formed in my head.

By the way, his name is Jim. And, Jim, thank you very much. Thank you for being there to make that comment. I'm incredibly thankful that I was there to hear it. That simple sentence changed my life.

The universe, God, whatever you're comfortable calling it, used Jim to answer the question I'd been asking for a long, long time through his comment.

You see, for a long time I'd been asking myself what I would do if I started my own business. I loved HR/Staffing, I enjoyed it very much. But..., I wanted something more. I wanted to do my own thing, generate and create my own income and not rely on someone else's company, vision, direction and goals. But I had no clue what I'd do. That is until I heard Jim's comment.

Write. It's what I love doing. It's one of my best talents. At that moment of discovery, I knew what my passion was, is. It was so clear it was almost blinding. Emotionally it was electric, energizing. The thoughts spinning like a hurricane in my head were almost deafening. It was clear. I had to write. I wanted to write. I'd do this.

Talk about fate. Shortly after my moment of discovery the staffing company I worked for succumbed to the Great Recession and was forced to close. Jobs for their temporary employees were scarce and a large client had stiffed them on a very large bill. However, that nail in their coffin was the also the key that opened my next career door.

I walked through that door, held my passion for writing by the pen in my hand (keyboard under my fingers in this case) and took off on a new journey. Ghost writing.

What I've discovered is that allowing your passion to show and embracing it will create opportunity. I know this sounds a little hokey, but it's true! Allowing my passion to lead me is why April invited me to write this chapter.

Ghost writing has allowed me to meet some incredible people. I've worked with new as well as experienced authors and playwrights. I've met presidents, CEO's, vice presidents, producers, philanthropists, activists, big thinkers, small thinkers, deep thinkers and those who did more doing than thinking. Different ghost writing projects have enabled me to meet all kinds of people.

I've reconnected with friends and associates from the past who are doing new things and are excited about the new path I'm on. I even got to learn about and work with a neighbor I've lived across the street from for the past almost a decade. Turns out he's into graphic design and a few of my projects required the help of a high quality designer.

My point here is… Following your passion will open doors for you as well as for those around you. Your passion will be contagious! Share it!

Well, I'm nearly at the end of my maximum of 2000 words. I have room to leave you with just a few additional thoughts…

Hindsight, being what it is, and that's invaluable… Hindsight has allowed me to realize that although it seems very difficult, finding your passion doesn't have to be hard. No, finding it doesn't have to be hard. For me I guess it was a case of, "Forest? I don't see any forest. All those damn trees are in the way".

Now that I realize it as my passion it's easy to see that it's been with me since I first learned how to form the letters of my name. Writing.

Following your passion does take faith, courage and bravery. Following your passion could mean filtering out all of the "no's" you'll hear or even tell yourself. It can be scary, at first...

Hey I lost my job with a very kind employer, steady salary and benefits for my family..., gone. I also had to face the fact that a decade + long career had been drastically changed by the plummeting economy and massive loss of jobs over the past few years. And forget the shoestring. My startup budget was more like knotted together pieces of broken thread. But those threads keep showing up and they knitted together a rather nice quilt.

Following your passion also takes, joy, happiness and love. Following your passion will bring you the "yes's" and positive support you need. It's fantastically exhilarating.

My advice on finding your passion, if you're interested, is...

Listen carefully. The universe may drop a comment on you when you least expect it. Your passion will burst in an almost uncontrollable moment of discovery. It will fill you like nothing ever has.

About the author:

Peter Gault: Who I am: Father, husband, dog and cat owner. I adore my family; they're the biggest part of me. I'm also an artist, creator, collaborator and enthusiast. I'm a lover of music, books, writing, stories and people. My passion shines through the creative process.

http://yourtopicalcontent.com/blog/?page_id=19

www.yourtopicalcontent.com

peter@yourtopicalcontent.com

I Found My Passion and It Only Took 24 Years!

By Izzy Kharasch

What I know about passion is that it is elusive. I know that in my case I had to really live and experience life before I could understand what my passion is. I know that a great part of my life has been a search not just to find my passion but to understand that I even have a passion. The reason I had trouble finding my passion is that I had to pass it by many times before I began to understand that what I was doing with my life was laying the groundwork that would allow me to appreciate my passion. I don't think I could have even told you what my passion was until I hit 40. The other thing about passion is once you finally understand what your passion is, everyone else wants to tell you why it's the wrong time to pursue it.

My Passion

My passion is for education. My passion is for learning and teaching. This comes from one of the worst students fortunate enough to graduate high school. In an odd way I have always considered myself very lucky, blessed even, because since 15, I have always felt that I was on the right road. I knew something was out there, just out of reach, just around the bend within my grasp if I could only understand what it was. I have appreciated every twist and turn that my life has taken along the way. Good or bad I always felt that these experiences were an intricate part of my learning process. It has been time and life experience that has allowed me to reflect, understand myself, appreciate my desire, and continue the search for my passion.

Not Letting Passion Pass You By

I have a brother who is about the smartest guy I know and he was great in school and unbelievable in math. When he went to college he majored in accounting because this is what his natural talent was. When he graduated he went to work for a big eight accounting firm and within a month he knew that this was not his passion. He could have been like a lot of folks and stayed in the job because he invested so much time and energy, it paid well and he was good at what he did. He made an unbelievably brave decision; he decided to go for his passion: medicine. This meant another five years of school and with more years of being an intern. Following his passion made him a different person. Many years later that passion for medicine is as strong today as it was when he told us he was quitting his job and going to med school.

Passion Begins As Fun

I needed to make money when I was 15 and a friend of mine hooked me up with a cook's job at Barnaby's Pizza restaurant. From the very first day I started working at Barnaby's I felt that I was in the right place. I thought it was the cooking that I enjoyed so much. On the third day of work I started what I would consider a small fire in the toaster. It seemed my manager felt that it was a bigger fire and a much bigger deal than I did. It was a good thing that he liked me or I would have been let go. On day four I began working a few hours a day washing dishes and the remaining hours bussing tables. I loved it all but I especially enjoyed being with the customers, hearing what they liked and why they enjoyed coming to Barnaby's. I knew that being a busboy or a cook or a dishwasher was not my passion but there was something about the hospitality industry that I was enjoying. It was the first time in my life that I felt that I was enjoyed something enough to want to pursue it as an adult.

Passion Is A Process

I knew that upper level education was not for me, so I decided to join the Army the summer that I left high school. I went to basic training and then I was sent to advanced training, another name for school. I really enjoyed the education I received in the military because it all made sense. Everything you learned directly related to your job. All of a sudden I loved math and science because I what I learned would be used every day as part of my job. When it was time to leave the service I decided to go to chef school. I knew that I was choosing a school that would not only add to my education but teach me what I really needed to know.

Changing Focus To Find That Passion

I followed that road, that passion out of school into a job as a chef. I loved being a chef but I was not passionate about being a Chef. The part of the job I loved most was training my staff. I appreciated the opportunity to teach something that I enjoyed. I knew that if I could communicate something that I get pleasure from rather than just the recipe, my staff would do better, be more creative and hopefully improve on what I taught them. I really got it! I loved the teaching and the training! I loved knowing that I was changing my employee's perspectives in terms of what they did and how they did it. I loved being able to send people back to their jobs more excited today than yesterday.

Passion Is All Or Nothing

I knew that I wanted to make training my sole focus, my career, my passion. It took a few years but I really understood that my talent was not cooking but teaching my passion: hospitality. At 28, I made the decision to give up a prestigious job as the Executive Chef of The Faculty Club at Harvard University. The job had great pay and great benefits but for me I knew that I would never be happy staying for those reasons alone.

I decided to talk to other companies and let them know I was available to be their director of corporate training. Alas, I was told time after time that I did not have enough experience. I did the last thing available to me, I hired myself! I started a company called Hospitality Works that would focus on training and consulting.

I knew I Found My Passion When.....

- I knew I found my passion when the word "No" motivated me to stick with what I was doing.

- I knew I found my passion when I told other people about what I was doing and most said that I should just get a full time job.

- I Knew I found my passion when after each training session all I could think about was how I could be more effective next time.

- I knew I found my passion when I was offered a part-time teaching position and my first thought was what an honor not how much it pays.

- I knew I found my passion when I searched for more ways to learn and more effective ways to teach.

- I knew I found my passion when, after more than 20 years I'm as excited today as I was when I taught my first class, trained my first group of employees and sat in a class that I had been looking forward to.

I Know This About Passion

- I know that finding my passion did not come easily.

- I know that finding my passion was worth the wait.

- I know that I look forward to talking about my passion with other people and when I do, it's as fresh and exciting to me now as it was when I just figured it all out.

- I know that I don't have a hobby because there is nothing that excites me more than looking forward to, creating or teaching that next class or conducting that next training.

- I know that I don't wish I had discovered my passion any earlier.

- I know that discovering my passion came to me when I was ready to understand it, accept it and then act upon it.

About the author:

Isidore S. Kharasch, owner and president, Hospitality Works, Inc. an operational foodservice consulting, training and management firm founded in 1987. Founder of Food Service

Professionals Network of Chicago, in April of 2009 Izzy also became a Certified Green Consultant allowing him to guide and direct businesses in becoming Green and Certified Green.

Sand Castles

By Doug Elwell

This is a fragment from a larger story of the same title. The full story looks at things a young man loses and the ones an old man finds. The reader won't find the word passion anywhere in this story, but I think it's there.

He was tired from the day before and the stresses of the morning. He didn't anticipate the emotional toll it would take to help Maggie make her final arrangements. With her home and resting in her room, he decided to go to the beach to just sit, relax for a while, alone. He threw a towel and a six pack of beer into a bag, crossed the road for a couple hours in the fresh air and sun. He went to the large driftwood log he claimed as his after it washed up months before. When he got there he settled onto his towel, opened a beer, took a long pull, then another to cut the phlegm in his throat. The rhythmic ebb and flow of waves on the sand relaxed him.

A sailboat on the horizon, inched its way north…how different things look from a distance…standing on the deck of that boat…I might be surrounded by a crew in chaos, but from here it looks serene, a thing of beauty and peace.

Before him on the beach, closer to the water was a young woman with two small children, little girls. The little girls chased the shallow remains of waves as they flowed back into the ocean then screeched with delight as the last foamy inches of the next wave chased them back up the beach.

The young woman sat on a towel trying to sun herself and keep a close eye on her girls at the same time. He judged her to be about the age Maggie was when he first met her back in Wichita many years earlier. He was sure life's final things were not on this young woman's mind this sunny day in the summer of her life as they were for Maggie; nor should they be. As he watched her he thought how different life must be for the young woman than it was for him and Maggie when they were in their youth. And he thought that was a good thing.

When he gave any thought about what life was like when he was young it seemed so primitive by today's standards. It hadn't been a really a long time, but the world had become a very different place since then. He thought it came down to expectations. His and especially Maggie's weren't the same as for the young woman on the beach. He was sure of that.

In his day dishes were washed by hand each night after a dinner cooked over a stove. He was content to live in a modest apartment furnished with handed down pieces from their parents or bought in second hand stores. Credit was hard to get and when it was available, people were afraid to use it except in emergencies. A new car would be nice, but the old beater parked out on the street ran okay, mostly; was paid for at least. They didn't expect to start out living like their parents did. It took them a lifetime to achieve what they had and he and Maggie expected they'd have to do the same. They were willing to forgo today for the promise of more and better tomorrow, perhaps after the next promotion. That was something to look forward to; someday, yes someday. Yes, it was all a matter of expectations and expectations are just that; not good or bad, just that. He looked at the young mother sunning herself on the beach with a sort of envy, you go girl.

He opened another beer and lit up a smoke. With Maggie near the end, he realized for the first time how much he had changed. He surprised himself how deeply he loved her, how much of himself he gave over to her and it was eating him up.

It wasn't always that way. He was a medic once a long time ago and learned to never get too connected. Those young boys came and they went and he couldn't carry them with him, he had to let them go without taking a piece of him with them. It was hard. He had to do it. Otherwise their pain would become his and eat him up. He was the last person many had seen in this world and he did his best to give them the peace he thought they needed. He held dying men close to press a human touch in their last moments. He looked into their eyes and said things to them he thought they wanted to hear, go in peace my brother. But he held back with Maggie for too long, learned his lesson too well. She was taking a piece of him with her, but now it was okay. He needed to feel the pain of losing her. It would be a small price to pay for so many years of her.

He opened his third beer and lit up another cigarette. He drifted back to the young woman and her children in the sun on the beach in front of him. Now they busied themselves building sand castles and he felt good about that because he could see the young mother was building more than sand castles with her daughters. They were building memories.

She was preparing them for their own lives and their own children someday. He knew that someday she would hurt when the girls would no longer be with her to build sand castles on a warm sunny day on the beach because he was losing Maggie and it hurt. He imagined that someday they would have their own children to take to the beach to outrun waves and make sand castles and laugh in the sun and he felt good about that too. The tide always comes in and washes them away as if they'd never been but the beauty of those days will remain in her heart. Soon he too would have the beauty of those days with Maggie in his heart.

He looked past the young mother and her little girls to the sailboat on the horizon. Maybe there was confusion on board, maybe the skipper was green. He didn't know. And from a distance he couldn't tell. Inching its way north, it would soon be beyond the horizon but in it's remembering he would find peace.

About the author:

Doug Elwell is a native Illinoisan who writes short fiction. He has studied at three universities and graduated from two. He is a veteran and now spends most of his days in a dirty, poorly lighted garret killing trees. He can be contacted via email at: djelwell@mchsi.com.

Passion!

By Mark Frietch

> "I can't imagine a person becoming a success
> who doesn't give this game of life everything
> he's got." - Walter Cronkite

Passion is more than taking pride in what you do. It is the feeling you get when you enjoy what you are doing. As I look back at successes in my life, whether it is personal or professional, I find the common denominator to be the passion for what I was doing at the time. One of my greatest passions is helping people. I'm not talking about sitting on some street corner waiting to help someone across the street. Nor is it holding open doors as people walk through. I assist people in helping them put their "Plan B" in to place. What is a "Plan B" you ask? That is easy. Plan B refers to the plan that everyone should have in finding the ideal job.

The Concept

As with any goal in life, you need a plan. You don't just jump on a plane and see where you land when it's time for that family vacation. You research the locations, check hotel prices, and reserve the air tickets or car. Nor do you just throw ingredients together and hope it comes out looking like a cake. You pull out a recipe. In the book Never Eat Alone by Keith Ferrazzi, he devotes a chapter to building a network before you need it. The plan B is a career plan that helps you get closer to finding your career passion.

A career plan should start by making a connection. Developing relationships with individuals who are in a position that, when needed will be able to provide direction and support to help you land on your feet. This is a key component in the plan B. Each person's plan will be different and will take some time to put together but in the long run, it will be worth every minute you devoted when you put your plan in place.

As I have done seminars over the past couple of months, I have had individuals come up to me and asked how a plan B is going to help them now. A plan B should not be a fall back. It is not just for those that are still employed. It is for any individual who wants to put themselves in a position where they don't have to go to sleep at night trying to figure out what is going to happen in the future. People that have been affected by layoffs say they need a plan A not a plan B. Plan A is making sure you are providing for you and your family. It is making sure that you are developing your brand and marketing it to the masses. Plan B should be about how you can position yourself in the future. If you have been affected by a layoff, downsizing, or whatever "pretty" name your company tried to call it; you should be in plan A mode. That doesn't mean you have to forget about plan B. Here are some things you can do to help you focus on your plan B.

Get Organized. Start Planning.

The first step in any plan is to get things in order. By organizing all your information, you will be able to readily access it when needed. Also, it will help you better keep up with things when they get hectic (and things will get hectic). The first thing you want to do to get organized is take a look at the environment around you. If you have a room that you use as an office, take some time clean out old files, shuffle documents around, or even rearrange the furniture. Sometimes moving things around will help clear your head for what you will need to focus on in the future. If you don't have a home office, start planning on where you can "set up shop" to do your work.

Now that your "workspace" is prepared, it is time to get started on defining your plan B. Pick a time when you will have little or no interruptions. Some of what you're about to do may take some time to really think about, but it will help you paint a solid picture for your goal. Make a list of things you liked and disliked about your last position. As you are making this list, write everything down. No matter how insignificant it may have been, whether you liked the atmosphere or hated working in a cube. This will help you start figuring out what you enjoy and want to look for in your next opportunity. Once you have completed that list, start making a list of things you would like to do in your new role. Don't limit it to what you did in your last position; make a true "dream job" list.

Once your "dream job" list is complete start making a list of everyone you know. This list should consist of family members, close friends, coworkers, and people from organizations to which you are involved. This list will be the foundation of your network. Find a location for these contacts. I suggest Microsoft Outlook, but any address book will work well. In this list you want to have their name, address, phone number(s), email(s), and the company where they work.

The last list you want to work on is the titles of some of your "dream jobs". Again, don't discount anything at this point. You want to be CEO of a Fortune 500 company, write it down. Once completed take a look at this list compared to your likes and dislikes and start whittling the list to those opportunities that fit with the other list. This list will be the starting point for the next step of the process, putting your plan B to use.

Now that you're organized, you can start putting your Plan B in to motion. Start by reaching out to your current contacts to see who they know in the field that you are interested. This will provide you with "warm call" opportunities. While you are reaching out to your contacts, sign up for a LinkedIn <http://www.linkedin.com> account. LinkedIn is a valuable tool for not only organizing your connections but to help find people who you may not know that are in the industry or field you are looking to transition into.

Connecting is Key

One of the things I have learned in my professional career is to never burn a bridge. Anybody that you have ever associated with could be a potential connection with someone you want or need to know. As you start connecting to individuals, don't beat around the bush, let them know specifically what you are after. Introduce yourself (you wouldn't believe how many times people call me and don't tell me who they are) to the individual and let them know how you are connected. Don't just go into a speech about your background. Ask to meet over a coffee, lunch, or drinks after work. Your focus is to genuinely build a relationship. The more relationships you form, the more opportunities will open.

Another way to find contacts and build relationships is using social networking sites like LinkedIn. If you do not have an account, stop and sign up. LinkedIn has been a valuable tool as I have grown my career. It provides you with another avenue of making a connection and building a relationship with key individuals. No matter what your Plan B is; you can find someone on LinkedIn who can help get you there. When you get logged on, fill out your profile completely.

This will help you start establishing a foundation on the network. This also increases your visibility when recruiters are doing searches. There are two types of networkers on LinkedIn. The first is an "open" networker. This individual accepts invitations from all sources. The other is a "closed" networker. They are more interested in developing deeper relationships with their connections. Neither type is wrong; it is just a personal preference on what you want to do. I personally am a "closed" networker. The benefit I gain from that is that anyone that is in my network will know who I am and be more willing to pass along information.

When looking to connect to individuals or groups, take some time to really decide if this is an individual you want to connect with. There are numerous groups on LinkedIn. They range from hobbies, political organizations, school clubs and corporate clubs. You may also find the same organization listed multiple times. Connecting on LinkedIn is as simple as sending an email. There is a section where you can send an introduction (from someone who is in your network), InMail (LinkedIn's webmail service) or by just getting connected (through past employers, schools, organizations, etc.). Any way you choose, it will walk you through the process. As you meet with these individual, ask them who they know that you could benefit from getting to know. This will help keep those warm connections flowing. But just talking to people is not enough. You need to make a name for yourself.

Get Out There

One of the biggest challenges for individuals in this workforce is being able to stand out. It's great to excel at your job, but if no one knows, does it matter? It is like the old saying, "if a tree falls in the woods and no one is there, does it make a sound? More and more people are finding creative ways to make themselves known. I just finished reading a book called *Me 2.0* by Dan Schawbel (highly recommend), he goes through some steps on how to help you differentiate yourself from the crowd. Tools such as blogs, video resumes, podcasting, and social networking allow you to grow your own personal brand, which can help you establish credibility among your peers.

I have found blogging to be far easier than I would have thought. It is a great way to provide your insight on a topic or topics of your choice. Once you start establishing credibility in the field you are choosing, people will start to look to you for guidance. This is critical in helping you to your end goal. As you start to follow these steps, there are a couple of things you need to keep in mind. First, as you get organized and start reaching out to people, you are going to become extremely focused. The key is not to forget about the people around you. Always make time for your family; after all, they should be your number one passion. I wish you the best of luck!

About the author:

Mark Frietch is a Recruiting Consultant and Social Media Coach. His experiences have been with developing and implementing recruiting strategies for Fortune 500 companies in various industries. Mark also works with companies and individuals to develop social media marketing and branding plans. You can view his blog and background at http://www.markfrietch.com.

12 Success Principles for Achieving Your Dreams by Accomplishing More in Less Time

By D'vorah Lansky

> "The greatest success in life is usually
> attained by simple means and the exercise of
> ordinary qualities. These qualities for the
> most part can be summed up in these words:
> common sense and persistence." - William
> Feather

When you think about success, what do you think about? There is a saying, "what you think about, you bring about". Are you focusing your thoughts on the things you want to create in your life or is your focus more on your challenges and difficulties? What would happen if you took the next 90 days to create new habits and allow more success into your life? Following, you will find 12 Success Principles for Achieving Your Dreams by Accomplishing More in Less Time. Read through these and select one or two Success Principles that resonate with you. You may want to make a note on your calendar or post a reminder by your computer, until these become newly formed habits. 90 days will come and go, where will you be? Go ahead; take the plunge by choosing one or more of the following Success Principles to put into action in your life! Here's to your success!

Success Principle #1 - Believe in the Power of Your Dream!

If you could have been or done anything, what would that be? You may want to spend some time writing and dreaming and remembering. What have you always wanted to do? What do you want to accomplish? What would you like to have happen in your life if you knew there were no limitations?

A key component for achieving your dream is for you to have a huge "Why". Give some thought to what your "Why" is. Is it to build the home of your dreams or take care of your elderly parents? Is it to send your children to college or build an addition onto your home to accommodate your growing family?

There is no limit to what we can accomplish if we have a big enough "Why". What is your Why for wanting more success in your life?

"Expect great things and great things will happen!"

> "If you think you can, you can. If you think
> you can't, you're right!" - Mary Kay Ash

Success Principle #2 - A Goal is a Dream With a Deadline!

To increase your level of success, have a clear idea of what you want to accomplish and set specific, time-sensitive, goals. When goals are set and action taken, things happen. Goals give you direction and purpose. Goals take you where you want to go.

Having a clearly defined goal is like having a destination for your journey in mind. Having a plan of action is like having a road map. Taking steps to develop your goals and plan of action will have a major and positive impact on helping you to get to where you want to go.

> "If you make the unconditional commitment
> to reach your most important goals, if the
> strength of your decision is sufficient, you
> will find the way and the power to achieve
> your goals." – Bob Conklin

Success Principle #3 - Your Success is Hidden in Your Daily Activity!

An excellent way to gauge whether an activity is one that will pave the way to success, ask yourself at any given moment, "Is what I'm doing right now taking me closer to my goals?" If the answer is "yes", then take a deep breath and take pride in your accomplishments. If the answer is "no", then take a deep breath and shift gears by refocusing your attention onto something that will take you closer to your goals and thus, your dreams!

The best use of your time is to prioritize people over paper. Are you making every moment count? Do you set a daily goal for the number of phone calls you'll make or appointments you'll hold each day? Something that you may find helpful is to remember that you cannot control your results but you can control your activity. By setting daily goals and tracking your activity, the results will follow.

> "How you spend your time is far more
> important than how you spend your money.
> Money mistakes can be corrected, but time
> is gone forever!" - David Norris

Success Principle #4 - Be Proactive - Not Reactive!

Do you begin each day with a schedule and a task list or are you more of a "fly by the seat of your pants" type of person? What would happen if you set office hours and carefully scheduled your time? When you have time scheduled for making phone calls or working on a project, consider screening your incoming calls. This can be very liberating and you'll be able to accomplish much more than if you are always reacting to other peoples' needs. By screening your calls, you can easily pick up the phone if there is a true emergency or urgent call. Return your calls during the time you have scheduled to do so. This way you can be totally present and not feel pulled in two directions. If this is a new concept for you, give it a try and prepare to be amazed at how much more you accomplish each day! There will be times when it is more effective to email the caller a reply. This can be most effective in the case of someone you are mentoring, as you can provide them an answer in writing that they can print out and keep.

Plan each day the night before by creating a "six most important things to do" list. This will give you a jumpstart on your day and keep you focused on what is most essential.

> "If you always do what you've always done,
> then you'll always have what you've always
> had." - Unknown

Success Principle #5 - Follow-up, Follow-up, Follow-up!

Your fortune is in the follow-up! How diligent are you about following up with people? Do you communicate mostly via email or do you take the time to follow-up with a phone call or a handwritten greeting card? Reaching out to people in a variety of ways can be very effective! Taking a few minutes a day to follow-up with at least one person can make a huge difference in your business!

> "Don't put off till tomorrow what you can
> accomplish today"- Josh Billings

Success Principle #6 - Let People Know You Appreciate Them!

When was the last time that you let your prospects, clients, friends and families know that you appreciate them? One of the greatest human desires is the need to be appreciated. What are some little things you can do to appreciate someone in your life, each day?

Here are a few ideas: Complement someone on an outfit they are wearing. Thank someone for their kindness or thoughtfulness. Send a heartfelt card to the first person who pops into your mind each morning. Purchase a dozen roses and hand them out to local store owners and clerks as you go about your errands.

What type of effect do you think this will have on others? The real gift is in how it will make you feel! The gift is in the giving. You may have heard the term "Give to Give". What that means is, you give with no thought of what you are going to get back. You can give to give in simple ways and in the scheme of things you will be also be enriched. What can you do today to let someone know you appreciate them?

"Appreciation wins over self-promotion every time!" - Kody Bateman

Success Principle #7 - Learn to Delegate!

Here's a reality check. Take a pad of paper and draw a line down the middle of the page so that you have two columns. At the top of one column write "things that only I can do". These are typically people centered activities such as attending networking events, following up with people and meeting with clients or prospects.

At the top of the other column write "things that I can delegate". Keep this pad at your side for the next three days and each time you do something, jot down that activity in the appropriate column. You will most likely be astonished as to how much you are doing that could easily be delegated to someone else. You may need to get over the fact that no one else can do as good a job as you can in certain areas. If you can delegate those activities, think of how much more you can accomplish by focusing on the activities that are best attended to by you!

Financially this is a very good investment on your part as you can earn much more in an hour than you will be paying to the person you are delegating projects to. The trick is to focus on income producing activities while they are working on your delegated tasks! What are the top three things that you'd love to delegate to someone else?

"Success comes in cans, not in can nots!" - Unknown

Success Principle #8 - People Support What They Help to Create!

By involving your family and/or your team in activities that will grow your business, you are setting yourself up for even greater success! People support what they help to create.

Let's talk about family involvement for a moment. We all get so busy and often prioritize business over family. What would happen if you were to schedule family time and prioritize this special time with the people that are most important in your life? Remember to let the phone machine pick up your calls when you are in family time.

A side benefit of this practice will be that your family will respect your office and phone calling time as they know that you respect and prioritize your time with them. Posting your office hours somewhere where they can see them is an excellent practice. You may want to color code your calendar so that it is easy for everyone to tell when you will be making your phone calls and when you'll be focused on family activities, etc.

What can you do today to prioritize spending special time with the people who are most important in your life?

> "Happiness is something to do, someone to love and something to look forward to!" - Unknown

Success Principle #9 - Take Control of your Life by Taking Control of Your Email!

Email is such a useful and important tool. It can also eat up hours of each day and become a major time waster. What would happen if you were to limit the number of times that you check email each day to once in the morning and once at night?

One solution is to have a primary email address for your business and a separate email address for any online subscriptions or newsletters. This will give you more control over your day and your week and make the information you've subscribed to easily available without cluttering up your primary email box.

Things were much simpler before email; we are able to accomplish amazing things with this valuable tool. The trick is to harness the power of this tool and not let it run our lives. Take charge of your schedule by checking your email only once or twice a day!

"Live each day to the fullest. Get the most
from each hour, each day and each age of
your life. Then you can look forward with
confidence and back without regrets!" - S.H.
Payer

Success Principle #10 - Take Care of Yourself and Feed Your Mind Daily

Which has a more long range, positive impact on your life, the nightly news or a chapter of a motivation book? By reading or listening to something inspiring or motivational, even if just for 10-15 minutes a day, over the course of a year you will have achieved the equivalent of having taken a course at a University.

In addition to what you feed your mind, be aware of what you are feeding your body. By eating high energy, healthy food and getting adequate sleep each night, you are setting yourself up for maximize success. Jim Rohn shares that the way to be truly successful is to work harder on yourself than on your business. What can you do to enrich your life and increase your success?

"What comes out of your mouth is
determined by what goes into your mind!" -
Zig Ziglar

Success Principle #11 - Take Time to Express Your Gratitude Each Day!

At the end of each day, write down three things that you are grateful for and three things that you did well that day. By doing this you will be focusing on and drawing to you more of the same. You may also want to write down one thing that you learned that day.

Keep this in a journal and write the date at the top of each page. This will be a fantastic record of your success journey. Prepare to receive miracles in your life. What are you most thankful for today?

> "Remember that your real wealth can be measured, not in what you have but in what you are" - Napoleon Hill

Success Principle #12 - Take Time to Smell the Roses!

Life is meant to be enjoyed! Yes, we need to focus and work hard in order to succeed. It is equally important that we take time to enjoy life; otherwise, what is it all worth? Consider setting aside one morning or evening a week just for you. You deserve this gift of time. What are some of ways that you can take time to smell the roses?

> "Success means having the courage, the determination, and the will to become the person you believe you were meant to be" - George Sheehan

There is a saying; you can begin a new habit in the middle of a bag of potato chips! Consider forming some new habits today and enjoy celebrating your success!

About the author:

D'vorah Lansky, M.Ed., is the bestselling author of Book Marketing Made Easy: Simple Strategies for Selling Your Nonfiction Book Online. D'vorah works with authors across the globe, through her book marketing coaching and training programs. Her flagship program on Virtual Book Tours has helped hundreds of authors promote their books. www.BookMarketingMadeEasy.com

Why Enthusiasm and Passion are Important and How to Create Yours

By Michelle Kabele

Recently at the World Economic Forum in Davos, Switzerland, worldwide political figures, business leaders and executives still had high expectations that the new American leadership could change the world in 2009. Wow! Nothing like carrying the weight of the world on your shoulders. But we must ask why – and how – in just about two years' time, a junior senator from Illinois can go from working in local and state politics to engaging world leaders to believe in the hopes, dreams, and vitality that can once again exist in not just the United States, but the world. It's all about enthusiasm and passion.

Whether or not you support the new administration, one thing is clear: President Obama invokes enthusiasm and passion in everything he does, from tackling the troubling economy and recession and foreign affairs to selecting the appropriate school for his daughters and even finding the best dog to become a part of the White House family. Despite some tough decisions, the President's approval rating is still extremely high. Many of those on the right have even said that although they don't necessarily support President Obama's policies, they hope he succeeds. The bottom line is that any great leader – whether the leader of a local community, a small business, a Fortune 500 company, or the leader of the United States – he or she must be passionate about the hopes for the future. The glass must always be half full.

When was the last time you woke up at 4 in the morning because you couldn't wait to get to work? If we compare this level of excitement to our younger school days, you may recall that it was easy to get up early on a Saturday when you knew you were going to the zoo, on a family vacation or playing with friends all day. But when Monday morning came along, you groaned, hit the snooze button and pulled the covers over your head to hide from the world a few minutes more. If you're a leader, every day should feel like a Saturday, and your customers, vendors and employees must "feel" this from you.

Let's take a look at how you can harness your enthusiasm and passion to become a great leader:

- Identify your passion. Hopefully it's what you do every day, both personally and professionally. And while one might argue that you can't feel passionate about everything all of the time, great leaders actually are. The difference is that great leaders choose what to become involved in and are passionate about their involvement. They don't get involved in everything that comes across their desk, however. They consciously select the ideas, projects and causes that are important to them and that will keep their dreams and goals moving forward positively.

- Lead with passion and others will follow. What makes you want to work even when you're exhausted and feeling burnt out? Whatever it is, let it show to your customers, vendors and employees. Whatever you love to do must be at your core being – what else is going to get you out of bed on a Monday morning after working 60 hours the previous week? If your followers understand what is important to you and can see the dedication and efforts you put forth, they will want to follow you to wherever it is you are leading them.

- Find teammates with the same passion as you. Whether it's a potential customer, a vendor, or an employee, having like-minded people on your team is only going to increase the enthusiasm level. If you all share the same core values, you will feed off each other to move the project or business idea forward. So build your team wisely. Talk with prospects about what you are passionate about and ask them what gets them out of bed every morning.

- Spend time with your people. There is nothing worse than a CEO that sits in meetings all day behind closed doors and who is invisible to his or her team, regardless of how those people fit into the big picture. As a leader, you must be accessible to everyone. Listen to what your customers have to say or what your employees think about the next product launch or service installation. If they know you truly care about what they think and that they are a part of the big picture, you will be able to create powerful change.

Articulate your passions and core beliefs often. The more you talk from the heart about what is at your core and how it relates to the task at hand, the more optimism and enthusiasm you'll inject into your team. In a way, you become a self-marketer of your visions and ideas, but at the root of that should be truth and reality. When combined, you have the formula for becoming a great leader.

During a recession, it's easy to see the gray skies. Searching for the silver lining can be difficult. But your followers will be looking to you to set the tone and be an example of the hope for what lies ahead. Having purpose and passion are critical to sustaining and even building business during tough economic times. By being engaged, passionate and excited about what you do, you will fuel the fire for those who choose to follow you to successful times.

About the author:

Michelle Kabele is dedicated marketing professional, Michelle Kabele Mkabele.wordpress.com has helped technology companies develop award-winning channel partner programs and strategies for 10+ years. She worked with Value Added Resellers throughout North America and thoroughly understands the realities and practicalities of planning and executing effective promotional, marketing, and sales campaigns.

The Passion Equation

By Sheri Bland, MSW

A walk in the woods, coffee with my friends, brainstorming a new idea....

What do you LOVE??

I LOVE when I get together with my girlfriends and we talk, laugh, cook up ideas and are fabulously brilliant; I feel understood. I LOVE talking with people about their business or seed of an idea. New ideas start to pop in my head about how to do it differently. A strategy formulates in my brain and the resources and vision begin to get laid out. I *LOVE* to laugh and have fun, to see the adventure and humor in situations.

I am DRIVEN to help people who are stuck, struggling or challenged in how to overcome a situation or relationship. I get DELIGHTED when they see hope, learn a new skill or find a way the overcome. I am DRAWN to young women who need encouragement or gentle mentoring to secure their way.

I LOVE to ENGAGE in conversation about how people's differences, communication and thinking styles can cause conflict and relationship problems. I love how to TEACH others how simple insights and new words can build bridges. I THRIVE when I'm with others who are forward, big-picture thinkers because I LOVE the synergy of a group thought process and new ideas. I ENJOY equipping kids to grow, learn their gifts, do their best and try something new to discover who they are.

I am WARMED when I can help enable someone to find out what they are good at and how to overcome the obstacles that prevent them from growing into all they were made to be. I am ridiculously COMPELLED to make lists, check them off, delegate, re-assess, and to keep looking at how to practically and efficiently get things done! I CRAVE the company of those who are authentic, caring, creative, accepting, strong yet vulnerable, moving ahead, responsible for themselves and going after all that life has (and who make me laugh)!

You could say I am passionate about all of that. Actually, I can feel my adrenaline rise and my creative juices flow…, even in talking about what I get excited about.

So if someone would ask you (or me): WHAT excites you? WHAT do you love to talk about and think about? WHAT gives you energy that drives and compels you? WHAT, even in the face of hard times or crisis, do you return to that continues to feed you and gives you LIFE? Or even, WHY do you like what you like? A key is this…what gives you LIFE?

If it feels like a noose, it probably isn't your passion. Does it bring life or death to you? What do you find yourself continuing to do through the many seasons and changes in life? Bingo. You've found your passion. Bingo again. I found mine.

Passion is what drives and compels you, what energizes and motivates you. It is what gives you life. It is the why and what that gives you a reason for being.

You are intrigued and can't help yourself but to do it in a variety of ways throughout your whole life. It is where you find your voice, your story, your reason for being, your stake in the ground, your… "I just really like to do it; it's who I am."

Vision is what you SEE for your life, or a situation, what you see for the future, what life would look like if only…

Mission is how you ACT on the vision you have, how you carry it out, the tasks and actions created to fulfill what you see or know in your heart. It's how you want something to be different. It is the venue or platform in which you fulfill your vision and passion.

<u>Core Value</u> is who you ARE inside, what the most important and basic beliefs that are unique to you, which you can't compromise on because it is who you are.

<u>Purpose</u> is the "WHY" of what we do.

The challenge, then, is how to find our passion when there is a transition or crisis of life, or a change in the season of life. How do we rediscover our passion when our perception is that we feel we've lost or misplaced it? When we feel we have no passion, no energy, or vision for the future how do we find it again? Passion is the fuel that keeps us going in this journey through life.

> "Deep in their roots, all flowers keep the
> light." –Theodore Roethke, American poet

I believe we are all born with a unique personality, gifts, style, dreams and passions that are matchless in the world. Throughout our life we grow, learn, fall, rise and create. Some days are filled with passion for a project, idea or for life; and other days…not so much.

Like the flower, the "light" we all keep is the promise that there is hope planted in us, that our life matters, that we have gifts, a destiny, and purpose to carry out. We all have a passion planted in us that cannot help but to bloom. It is in our DNA just as that flower is encrypted and kept in the plant until it is time.

How do I find it? How do I fuel it and allow space for my passions to keep growing as I go through the mundane, the crises and trials of life? How does the flower bloom amidst the desert, apathy or exhaustion?

I bring us back to: what excites you? What, when you talk about it, makes your speech go faster? When you talk with others, what gets your wheels turning and gives you energy, even when other parts of life bring you down? What fuels you? That's it! That's your passion. *It doesn't leave you.* Just like a flower can never be forgotten or extracted from the root…the flower IS the reason for the root, the most intrinsic part. The flower can seem like it is gone or missing, dead or lifeless. To that I would say, perhaps this is a season of winter in life. Or maybe there is a change or transition you are adjusting to.

Remember that change isn't a bad thing; it's just that something is very different now and you are called to create new responses and thought processes. That takes a whole lot of energy. Change and transition require a "re-do" to establish and adjust to "the new normal". Burnout can occur in which exhaustion or apathy take over. An overall look at life to do a re-alignment and tune up is necessary so you can run well again.

Passion can be confusing because sometimes we think that we need to have work that uses our creative expression for our passion to be ignited. Not so. Sometimes we are paid for what we are passionate about, and sometimes we aren't. I would prefer to get paid for what I am passionate about. However, often we get paid for what we are good at, or have done in the past or what we can do well enough and can tolerate.

Our passion must then take root to break ground in other places in life to find the light and to bloom and express itself in new ways. Passion is not the same as a hobby or interest, which we do to relax. We can feel passionate about a hobby or leisure pursuit; however, in talking about finding and igniting our passion, we look for that which gives our life meaning.

What's my passion and what am I passionate about? That feels hard to articulate. If you would ask me: what am I excited and enthusiastic about, what gives me energy and what do I keep returning to? Now, I can talk about *THAT*.

In training a group of leaders, we as a group identified what were our core values, mission, vision, gifts and passion. I came up with a summary statement. It helped me to narrow down who I am, what compels and feeds me and how I relate to my world through my uniqueness. This, then, is Sheri's passion in a nutshell....

"I encourage others to see opportunities
through creative thinking and practical
solutions, and I spread enthusiasm by
engaging others to see a hopeful future."

It took me a while to narrow down who I am and what my life is into one sentence! Yet I do feel like that articulates who I am. I have expressed this passion in different arenas and groups, in changing life seasons and settings, throughout my life.

I express this passion as a coach, trainer, friend, business consultant and administrator. Professionally, I am currently "energized" by empowering and equipping those who want to grow their business and be on the cutting edge. Personally, I am fueled in this season through encouraging new moms, mentoring teens and injecting hope and life into women's lives. I just want to be where the new ideas and growth are, so that happens in many places!

Now you try. Far be it from me to sum up your life in an equation. Then again, it sure beats reading multiple self-help books to figure it out.

What do you love to do? What excites you, gives you energy? List two Passions (Passion=Ps)

What do you feel strongly about? What do you believe in strongly? (Core Value=CV)

Where do you like to spend your time and with what kind of people? Where have you seen success? What behaviors of yours have been affirmed by others? (Mission=M)

Why do you do what you like to do? (Purpose=Pr)

How would you like to see things be different or change because of what you can do? (Vision=V)

Once you fill in the answers to those questions, you can begin to envision what is your passion. It is already in you and in your life. You just need some tools, a process and a way to articulate what is there so you are able to identify it within yourself.

Remember that darn root has to push through a lot of hard dirt and manure to break through the soil to allow the tip to start its blooming into the flower.

Here goes… Fill in the blank, just like elementary school.

I really like/love to do _____ (Ps)

I get lots of energy when _____ (Ps)

I feel strongly about and want to take action about _____ (CV)

What I do well that is unique to me _____ (M)

Why I like to do it, the reason I do it is_____ (Pr)

What I would like to change or see for the future _____ (V)

If I do (verb) _____ with (who/what) _____, then I'll realize (outcome) _____.

Now you've created your Passion Equation: *(Ps+CV=M)* + *(Pr+V) =YOU*

You are now on your way to finding and igniting your passion!

It's time to *LOVE, EMBRACE, BE ENGAGED IN, ENJOY, GET EXCITED ABOUT, BE COMPELLED BY, THRIVE ON* and *INTRIGUED WITH* the things that give us *PASSION.* Discovering your passion is discovering yourself. Once you understand who you really are, you'll discover, through your passion, the true joy of being alive.

About the author:

Sheri Bland, MSW, is a business strategist, trainer and coach with 30 years experience in professional organizations and businesses. She provides training, organizational improvement, workforce development and management consulting. Her strengths lie in creative and practical resolution to the obstacles that occur with individuals and organizations. P: 815-477-3775 sheriabland@gmail.com http://www.linkedin.com/in/sheribland http://www.sheriblandsolutions.com/

RAIDers of the Lost Sale – A Journey to Business and Personal Success

By Andy Hughes

Back in 1997, I was employed by a global manufacturing company based in the UK, which was undergoing a major business merger. Through hard work and spectacular results I was offered a challenging position within the newly formed company. The role involved a bid for the largest consumable product contract in Europe and, after only three months and making an instant impression on the directors of the business I was charged with taking responsibility for the whole account.

After successfully being awarded supplier status for this contract I set about developing a plan which would challenge the largest company in the world in its field and successfully win millions of pounds worth of business. Within 9 months I had single handedly positioned the company as market leaders within the contract. At the beginning of the campaign the sales ratio was 1 of our sales to 89 of theirs (1:89), after nine months the ratio was 4 of our sales to their 1 (4:1).

Following this success I went onto re-negotiate the contract for another three years with the same company and secured another three-year term some time later, when I moved to another company within the same market sector. During this ten-year period I also went onto secure an exclusive multi million pound contract to supply consumables to the largest private healthcare group in Europe for a period of five years.

The success achieved in 1997 brought with it a flurry of questions, not just from company directors, but also from my client and many of my competitors. How did I do it? Pre 1997 I had personally funded all of my sales training, attending as many conferences and seminars as my commitments would allow. I also read more books than I can remember on the subject of Sales and Marketing. However, after reading *How To Win Friends and Influence People* by Dale Carnegie early in my career I developed a sales strategy (Traffic Lights) which formed the basis upon which I won major contracts within business sectors such as Aerospace, Defense, Catering and Leisure and the Public Sector (Government and Education Contracts). The book became my bible, and I encouraged everyone to buy a copy and read it.

So what was behind all of this success? Post 1997 I created RAIDers of the Lost Sale-with the emphasis on the beginning, RAID, which stands for Research, Appraise, Indentify and Do. In the earlier days of my career I read a vast number of sales related books, all detailing how individuals had achieved success and the methods and principles they used. But was it possible that one person had all the answers? Do strategies work the same for everyone or just for the individuals who design them!

What I did uncover was that during my own periods of success there were four ever present elements. Research and lots of it, Appraising (relevant to my goal), and Identifying the opportunities and the methods by which I would achieve my goals. If you carry out the first three elements and don't Do anything with it, then you are likely to fail. When I presented RAID to my business colleagues for the first time I was amazed to find that not many of them actually conducted detailed research, they only carried out appraisal when things were not going according to plan and although they were identifying, they were only looking at the elements of what was or had gone wrong. Yes they were all DOing, but no-one was experiencing the level of success they desired.

When we mention the very word research, most people visualize a be-speckled person at a bench looking into a microscope or some person locked away in a room chalking one scientific formula after another onto a blackboard, however, this clearly isn't the case. The correct research will deliver the right results. It did for me on more than one occasion and there was not a microscope in site. As an example, research needs to be broken in pieces, similar to the "who, what, where, when and why" concept employed by many sales people. How and what we use to research has progressed rapidly with the introduction of the worldwide web. Back in the latter parts of the 1980's and 1990's the internet was very different and the main sources of research were paper journals (industry specific) and the local library.

Appraising information gained from your research is another key element. Is what you have enough? Do you need more information? If so what? And where can I find it? Appraisal should follow a similar format to that which you would employ during a career review. What is good? What else is needed? How you can do it better? What are your goals? During appraisal you should start to identify where your opportunities are, how you can put them into action and who you should action them with and when. Identifying is like a shopping list, you need to buy all the right ingredients to bake the perfect cake….right!

The Do, whether designing a plan, creating a strategy, or delivering a marketing campaign, Do is about decision and delivery. Do nothing and nothing happens. Do the right things and great things happen and you don't need to have 30 years of experience or a degree in economics to be successful. Keep the four elements in mind and never try to cut corners.

One of the most fascinating aspects of RAID is that we use the same four elements everyday of our lives. We do this subconsciously and sometimes within a matter of micro-seconds. To illustrate, here are some examples:

1. You go to a shop to buy a new television: you look around and ask questions (Research), the shop assistant answer's your question(s) and you think about the response (Appraise). Then you ask some more questions, you get more answers regarding its specification, sound quality, picture quality, split screen etc, and you think again (Identify) based upon your must have's

from buying a new television....and guess what comes next, yes, you guessed it (Do) as in decision time.

2. Even with relationships whether they be social or work, you introduce yourself and begin asking questions (Research). With the replies you start to (Appraise), do I like this person? etc. After a while you begin to (Identify) common ground and then if everything fits, you move the relationship forward (Do). Heck, we do all four during courtship, we just do it subconsciously.

So where does all of this fit into the RAIDers of the Lost Sale?

Back in the last millennium the big screen movies were all about action and adventure. Do you remember Indiana Jones and the Raiders of the Lost Ark? In the movie there was a quest for secrets, answers and buried treasure. Before my success in the mid nineties I was also on a quest, to find the secrets to sales and personal success. RAIDers of the Lost Sale was born, a simple but effective approach to sales and personal success using Sales and Marketing principles at it core.

My passion has always been sales and marketing and I have found a unique way of translating it into all aspects of social, working and personal relationships,

What of the future? Well, research will still be done no matter what technology. We will still appraise to find the answers, and we will still be identifying ways to make progress and whatever level of technological advances (or not) we will always be doing. I believe RAIDers of the Lost Sale will be around for some time yet, however, I do plan to revitalize and keep it relevant with current and future trends.

I continue to use sales and marketing as a medium for organizations and individuals to better understand the connection it has on a social, personal and business level and published an ebook *Career and Jobseeker Mapping* to help individuals understand the commercial value they have and how to market that value to gain employment, its free, so feel free to visit my Facebook page http://www.facebook.com/careerjobseekermapping/ to download a copy.

On closing, remember one very important value:

> "Nobody knows everything, but everybody can learn."

About the author:

Andy Hughes is a Sales and Marketing consultant based in Derby, UK. He uses sales and marketing as a medium for organisations and individuals to better understand the connection it has on a social, personal and business level. Andy can be contacted directly at Sales and Marketing Consulting ahsalesandmarketing@gmail.com and through LinkedIn www.linkedin.com/in/andyhughes0.

Transformation to Achieve Fulfillment

By Julia Gorelik

We often live our lives day by day, not planning for the future or considering the after affections of our decisions and choices. What motivates us to make a positive impact in the world? What will it take for us to look at the big picture and transform short-term decisions into long-term results? Perhaps the true question is what legacy would you like to leave behind? How would you like to be remembered and are you on the path to achieving this?

Let's first uncover the challenges people face in creating a life purpose or goal. This could include the changes we make as we grow up. As we get older and wiser, our views and priorities change. The career we once thought was perfect for us may now be a nightmare and rediscovery or re-educating ourselves to a new career is necessary. Then family priorities change. At one time, we thought we'd get married by a certain age and then have kids by a certain age and suddenly we find ourselves single (no kids or spouse in sight) when we had already planned to be done having kids. So, these variances between our plan and reality kick in. What now? How much control do we really have?

There's no guarantee in life that everything will work out your way. On the contrary, life will always challenge you and it's your job to overcome and achieve. So, in the big scheme of things, how do we create the legacy desired with all the unexpected variables? Well, what do you have control over? Starting out easy is the only way to put things into perspective and gain a hold of life. If you want to be remembered as a generous person, when was the last time you helped a friend or gave to a cause? If you want to be remembered as honest, have you lied or mislead anyone lately? If you want to be remembered as an entrepreneur who employed 100s of people, what is your big business idea and what's the plan of attack to help get you there?

Bottom line: We can live life day by day, make decisions for the moment and not consider the repercussion of our actions. However, before we know it, 20 or 30 years will go by and we'll ask, "Where did the time go?" Why put yourself in that position? How rewarding would it be to create a legacy, know how you want to be remembered and start living that life today?!?

The question now becomes... What is your dream?

Having the desire to be someone, accomplish something and be remembered as you intended all starts with setting personal and professional goals and setting out to achieve them. Once that concept is understood, the question becomes: "How do I stay focused on accomplishing goals without losing sight of the purpose and not getting distracted by life's struggles and constant changes?" This is a very common concern and often negatively affects staying on track to achieve a goal. Here are some suggestions:

1. What is the goal? Focus on what motivated you to create it. Is it a health concern, financial concern, or personal goal? Be aware of the importance and positive changes that will occur when this goal is achieved.

2. Place a reminder around you. Either cut out a picture of the ideal body you want, home you want to live in or career you desire. Whatever the goal, it's important to see it on a consistent basis so it's not forgotten. Place it somewhere in your home or office where it's visible; when you pass by the picture, visualize yourself already accomplishing that goal. Experience the feeling every time you see the picture. In order to manifest your dreams and desires, you must believe that they can occur and see your life changed because of them.

3. Break down the goal so it's measurable and achievable, so you can work towards it on a daily/weekly/monthly basis. Set a reminder for yourself every month to track your success. You can easily create a spreadsheet to measure how far along you are.

4. Find an accountability partner with whom you'll share your progress. Therefore, make sure this person is aware of your short term goals in order to achieve the ultimate long term goal. This way, your accountability partner can make sure you're on track.

5. Have a backup plan in case you fall behind. Are you willing to accelerate things one month to make up for a previous month's shortcomings? If so, make sure your accountability partner is aware of how to motivate you.

6. Celebrate the small successes. If you've worked hard for several weeks/months or accomplished half the goal, reward yourself!

7. Make sure to have fun; create a game out of it. Track and share your progress, struggles, etc. with your accountability partner. Allow your partner to support you and make suggestions.

8. Make sure to remember the reason you created the goal and visualize achieving it every time you lose focus or purpose.

9. Good luck and enjoy!!!

The process and challenges associated with accomplishing goals also involves a level of personal development and introspection. Introspection involves overcoming your nature to step outside your comfort zone and take risks with potential rewards that will forever change your life. Our belief systems are often the cause of the results in our life. If we have an association that money only comes to people with a certain level of education, then we'll never have money without that education. Given this level of consciousness, how do we change our belief systems to empower us and improve our lives? How do we change our behavior or the situations around us? Remember, the only thing you have control over is yourself; create the possibility to have everything. What would that look like? How would that negate the belief system instilled in you? Are you willing to look within, do some work and change yourself and the outcomes in your life? If so, you must start by doing some self reflection and have the willingness to be aware and make changes. Here is a step by step process:

1. Identify what is hard... What pushes your buttons? When do you feel immediately reactive or defensive?

2. Acknowledge that this situation is placed in your life for a reason, to help you develop and be the best individual you were destined to be in this lifetime. This situational test is to help you realize that there's something you need to learn to help yourself grow and develop.

3. Identify your reaction... Do you feel like lashing out? Are you upset, hurt, mad, angry, frustrated, or do you feel helpless? Why are you experiencing this? Would others react this way? Are you taking it personally? What are your assumptions as it pertains to the situation?

4. Restrict. This might be very difficult but you must stop yourself from reacting and allow the process to happen and reflect on what went wrong. How did this situation arise? Don't take things for granted; appreciate the opportunity to change through this experience. This is an opportunity to learn from your own experiences, change your reactions and become a better person. What is your blockage?

5. Deal with the situation differently and change your consciousness! Stretch yourself by changing the results. Be aware of your reactive nature and what is causing this reaction within you. From this point forward, appreciate this learning experience and be prepared in the future to handle things differently.

The definition of insanity is doing the same thing but expecting different results. In order to change the results in your life, changing your actions, reactions and routine are the only ways to successfully influence the outside factors that influence your happiness and sense of fulfillment. So start by looking within and being aware of how you view and handle situations in your life.

About the author:

Julia Gorelik, Certified Professional Coach from ICA (International Coach Academy), grew up in the northern suburbs of Chicago and realized early on that her desire to help people was a part of her life's purpose and where she received the most fulfillment. Julia Gorelik offers complementary trial sessions, contact her at (312) 638-0888, Julia@Fulfillingfuture.com or her website: http://www.fulfillingfuture.com.

Passion Action Plan: Defining Our Personal Mission Statement

By Sandra Larkin

Today, we are world of many choices. So many, that it causes stress and anxiety to even attempt to make a choice for fear it's the wrong one. If you enter "find your passion" into any internet search engine, you'll find hundreds of websites, blogs, books and organizations that will help us do just that. How do we break it down into a simple formula to help us get where we're going without traveling through minefields that lead us to nowhere?

Who am I? Why am I here? What do I do next? These are questions I continue to ask myself along my own personal journey. Trying to define our passion can be a complicated process. It begins with building and maintaining a personal mission statement, which guides our direction, decisions and experiences to a higher purpose. At the end of the day, we can take our activities and clearly measure how much in alignment we are to our passion. We can bounce our life up against this statement for balance and purpose.

A personal mission statement …

- Comes from within us. It's a journey and a process. It's not a race. Today we want our dreams, desires and success in an instant. Basically, add water and poof, "success", without going through the process of pain, happiness and frustration. It's really about waiting, feeling and having it come from the inside of us.

- We discover it, we don't decide it. We go through life liking this and hating that. What have we discovered about past choices and associated feelings? What are our core values (i.e. trust, integrity, compassion, organization, family, etc…)? What excites and inspires us each day and not just for the moment?

- What we want to do, not what we should do. Other people unknowingly place their passion and purpose like a boulder in the road of our journey. We need to keep in perspective that it's about us and no one else. If we continue to allow others to direct our lives with even small choices, then we end up unhappy, negative, frustrated, and most of all, directionless.

- Focus on past life experiences. How do we know in what ways that our past can expel us forward or drop us into a sinkhole? Creating a timeline of our positive and negative life experiences alerts us to how our passion may look in the positive and negative mode. In other words, what to move towards and what to move away from.

In addition, personal mission statements should be...

- Short and to the point. Not a novel or a never ending paragraph.

- Broad and mysterious. Where our personal and professional lives can cohabitate.

- Should not be goals or goal related. Goals are too easily reached leaving us without anything to shoot for throughout our lifetime. In addition, we would need to continually reinvent our personal mission statement or possibly ourselves.

Let's begin our journey using a step by step process. This helps us avoid confusion and gets straight to the heart.

Passion Action Plan

1. The Tough Questions. Begin by honestly answering these questions.
    - I am here on earth to …?

    - My purpose in life is …?

    - The most important thing in life is …?

These questions get right to the heart of who we think we are, what we do and what we value as important. What we value comes from our core values, which are intrinsic to how we make decisions on a daily basis. Looking at our past decisions we should see what we value (i.e. family, friends, money, things and stuff) and how it made us happy or feel unsettled.

Let's see how these questions look from another person's perspective? They are short, broad, and mysterious and not goal oriented. Can you tell which career they are?

I am here on earth to …?

"I am here on earth to teach children the skills they need to be successful in the world and to help them awaken to the joys of the written word."

Answer: Elementary school teacher; Sunday school teacher; English teacher.

My purpose in life is …?

"My purpose in life is to protect others and to give them a sense of safety and security."

Answer: Parent; Police Officer.

The most important thing in life is …?

"The most important thing in life is to learn about love, cultivating an intimate relationship with another human being."

Answer: Nurse; Therapist; Minister; Doctor

Now answer the three questions honestly. Don't be surprised if it takes a few days or weeks to come up with the answers. We really need to think and feel before writing.

- I am here on earth to …?

- My purpose in life is …?

- The most important thing in life is …?

2. Putting It All Together
    Put your three written answers together into one paragraph. This is our framework in building and refining our personal mission statement.

    "I am here on earth to teach children the skills they need to be successful in the world and to help them awaken to the joys of the written word. My purpose in life is to protect others and to give them a sense of safety and security. The most important thing in life is to learn about love, cultivating an intimate relationship with another human being. "

    Our passion will arise out of our personal mission statement like a phoenix from the fire. The fire of lifelong experiences, desires, success and failure.

3. Getting To The Passion
    What does passion look like from our personal mission statement? Let's drill down into our example.

    Passion List

- Educate others on the "how to's" of being successful which includes adults and children.

- To change careers and become:

    - a law enforcement or government official

    - an attorney

    - a healthcare advocate

    - health care professional

    - teacher (children or adult)

- Discover the joy and fulfillment of missionary work

- Volunteer at our community food bank or homeless shelter

- Volunteer to read to children at the local library

• Plus more …

4. What's next?

Each day gives us an opportunity to develop goals moving us towards our passion. Write a list of attainable goals to begin the pursuit.

For example, if we were to pursue the passion of "volunteering to read to children at the local library", our goals maybe:

• Call the local library and see what children's programs are already available.

• What are the days of the week and times this takes place?

• Is it possible that this can take place in the evening or on a Saturday/Sunday?

• Think of a theme to include. For example, dress up like a character from a storybook, include a dog to read to, create a signature ending that children will remember.

• Meet with the librarian to find out how you can participate in children's programs already available.

• Plus more …

5. Just do it! (Nike)

Lace up our running or walking shoes, grab your action plan and GO! We need to use our time wisely and learn to say "NO" to those events that will distract us from what's important in our life. Saying "NO" is not negative. It's a personal tribute to ourselves and a declaration to others that our goals and mission are not in alignment with what is being asked of us at this time. Maybe later but not right now.

Sandra Larkin, CWPM - My Personal Story

In 2005, I resigned a corporate position, in an effort to right size failing health. At that time, I had no clue I was starting the journey to find my own passion. It's been fun, exciting, stressful and frustrating all at the same time. Anything worthwhile usually is.

Out of the *Passion Action Plan* process my personal mission statement came....

"Helping people be successful and businesses make money."

Since 2005 I have said "NO" to plenty of opportunities. If what was being asked on a personal or professional level was not in alignment with this statement, I respectfully declined. Was the other person always happy? Not really. I came away knowing that what I was doing was in alignment to my passion and contribution to life.

Here are a few of the opportunities that I said "YES" to that help me pursue my passion.

- Form a publishing company.

- Published a book, *Healthy Profits: The 5 Elements of Strategic Workplace Wellness*.

- Collaborated and project managed the book with 25 other global authors.

- Pursue my desire to become a Dale Carnegie Facilitator. Currently, I coach and train organizational leaders on leadership skills increasing the people profit as well as the bottom line.

- Awarded the honor of being entered into the 2008/2008 Cambridge "Honors Edition" of *Who's Who Among Executive and Professional Women*.

- Obtained a Certified Wellness Program Manager degree.

- Formed a wellness organization "UeQuest, Inc." with two other health professionals.

- Personally coached some pretty impressive people who went on to pursue their passion and are highly successful as well as happy.

- Became a time management guru helping others get their time under control to pursue their passion.

- Plus more.....

Can you do this? The answer should be "YES!". Will you do this? The answer should be "YES!" but that's up to YOU.

I personally believe you can find and pursue your passion with positive expectancy and charismatic energy. All you need is to ....

"Just do it!" – Nike

About the author:

Sandra Larkin, President Sandra Larkin Wellness Strategies, LLC, is an international motivational speaker on workplace health and wellness. Professional qualifications include: Certified Wellness Program Manager, Intrinsic Health Coach, multiple Corporate Facilitation Certifications and Bachelor of Science in Business Administration. Sandra has over 25 years of leadership, time and project management experience.

Follow Your Passion Even Through Change

By Lynette Phillips

> "In this world nothing can be said to be certain, except death and taxes." - Ben Franklin

I'm sorry Ben but there's another life certainty; change. Life is constantly throwing new challenges in our path; these challenges call for changes, which mean that when it comes to our passions we'd better be flexible.

Case in point: When I finished high school, like millions of other graduates, I was college bound. I dreamed of books, history, research, teaching/sharing; i.e. my passions. Life change number one was just around the corner. Instead of college I got married and started a family.

How could I integrate my passions into a life that was so much different than the one I had planned? I unexpectedly found ways to combine the history, books, research and teaching/sharing passions that I had dreamed of with a budding family. Then even more remarkably I was able to continue blending my passions even through other life changes.

The methods and questions below have helped me throughout the years. Try applying them to your current life changing event and see how they can help you.

Q & A time – no matter how much you love your life and the people in it there are times you find yourself in a rut. You've lost your passion for your life - living other people's lives alone just isn't enough – there's something missing. It's time to do something.

I started by asking myself questions.

"What has the driving force in life always been?"

"What caused me to find new challenges?"

"What do I love doing more than anything else?"

Curiosity - a wonderful motivator.

Anytime I'm curious about something I have to find out the "when, where, why, how and who" connected to the event, occasion or person.

When a question would pop into my head, I'd be off to the library. (Fortunately the toddler I dragged with me to the library enjoyed the children's section.)

Obviously research is connected to curiosity and research and books go together; they also help satisfy my love of learning. My love of research was so strong – then and now – that I applied it to my love of history. My husband and I even toyed with writing local historical fiction short stories. We never published them but it was fun to write them.

Volunteering – As my daughter reached school age I entered that world. I volunteered in the classroom, the school library, for the scout troop and on the sports field.

I found that I loved to see the kids discover new things and to spend time with them. I was able to tune into my teaching and sharing interests. I shared my love of books and reading at the library and was a teacher's aide, reinforcing the teacher's lessons and performing tutoring duties.

I had found another way to pursue my passions!

"Just Do It!" - There are times when you find yourself in a situation that you think couldn't possibly lead you into a passion but sometimes you don't have a choice about life changes so you "Just Do It!" as Nike says.

For me this involved family illness. I was determined to understand everything that was happening. I wanted to know as much about the illness as possible, the treatment, what to expect in the future, what may have been the cause, everything. This may seem a bit gloomy but I applied the "Just Do It!" viewpoint and started with books and the library again.

Set Goals - If you're wondering why I didn't put the Internet to good use, it's as simple as it wasn't available. By the 1980's everyone was asking computer questions though. There didn't seem to be anyone to answer those questions except computer technicians. Most of the people that I knew with questions didn't want anything to do with the guts of the thing – they just wanted to know how to use it and get it to do what they wanted.

I decided to become the 'go to' person for computer use questions primarily for my own enlightenment. There weren't any classes available for what I wanted so it was back to books and the library. I did it! I became the company computer guru and even received questions from outsiders. Later I decided to teach computer use classes since everyone had started calling me to answer their questions anyway.

Step Out Of Your Comfort Zone - It was about this time that my daughter graduated and decided to leave home. She married, had three kids and then divorced. After the divorce she and the kids moved in with my husband and me.

My daughter was trying to work and go to school at the same time while being a full-time single mother. I helped out but time had moved ahead 20 years. It was time to move forward not backward by raising another family. I found myself in a rut again.

Another life change had come about. I loved my grandkids, spending time with them, caring for them and watching them change and grow but it was time to forge ahead and not to do the same ol' thing. I still helped out but this Grandma went back to school part-time.

My college dreams hadn't died. I had picked up a class every chance I got and now I decided to add more college level classes to meet California's state requirements for paralegals and legal assistants so I could research legal cases.

A new career as planned was not in the cards though. True, I worked in the legal field briefly but then a series of orthopedic surgeries became necessary. Afterward I wasn't myself anymore. I started getting depressed during the long recovery period. My husband saw what was happening and went to the library. As I was just staring out the window one day he dumped a stack of books on the bed and told me to stop feeling sorry for myself. I'd always complained about not having enough time to read so now was my chance. I started consuming - a very apt word - three to five novels a week.

My bones knitted as I read and spent quality time with my grandkids who had taken it on themselves to take care of grandma. My granddaughters returned to school but their 18-month old brother continued with his 'job'. As time went on we were able to add activities to our schedule. I searched out age appropriate websites – yes, they exist – and his computer lessons started. I was reading and teaching but it still wasn't enough. I decided to start blogging about what I read.

The blog was highly successful; I developed online relationships within the literary world with authors, publishers, editors and even book marketers besides those with readers and I was soon seen as an expert in the book world. I started getting questions about editing, writing and book marketing.

My first thought was I'm not qualified to help these people. One of the authors/publishers I had developed a relationship with asked me "why not"? I thought about it and decided she was right. I had basically been reading, studying, learning and writing all of my life. Add to that the years of marketing experience I had built while trying to 'find' myself as an employee, business owner and real estate professional and all I needed to do was redirect my thinking.

My assembled passions had led me to a new, much larger passion. I am now considered a book marketing expert, I write and of course read and study constantly to stay current.

By living my passions I have finally found my niche in life!

About the author:

Lynnette Phillips finds passion in helping authors market their books, writing and staying abreast of the inner workings of the literary world. She has shares her marketing tips via her blogs and books and is a frequent guest blogger and interviewee. Visit her at http://everydaybookmarketing.com/ or find her books on Amazon.com in the Kindle Store.

The Road to Finding Your Passion

By Linda Eenigenburg

The road to finding your passion does not come with a map. The good news is you don't need one. Different people have different destinations.

So often we think of passion in the romantic sense only. While this does exist, passion can be a part of so many areas of our lives. It can be work, family, love, even retiring and living out your years on a sailboat. But how do we find our passion?

Oh, the dreaded status quo! How easily we are fooled into believing (and not questioning) that there is one best way to live our lives. That is a sticky wicket, a trap we can so easily fall into. We grow up, graduate college, get married, have children, retire with a pension, and well...you know the rest.

While there is absolutely nothing wrong with living the status quo, where is your passion? If you have no passion in your life, you are missing the journey of a lifetime! But again, how do we find it?

The road to finding your passion can be a bit bumpy, perhaps littered with obstacles. Everyone experiences this on their journey to finding passion, but it's what we do when we reach one of those barriers that can set us apart from the pack. Picture this; you are walking down a dirt road, searching for your destination and not quite sure how to get there. It's muddy. It's dirty. It is bumpy, with ruts and grooves. You worry that you are going to twist your ankle or run out of food and water and question if it is worth the risk to continue on. At this point, it is so easy to give up on your destination, thinking that this is just too hard, too messy and perhaps even too painful.

When we reach a tough stretch of road, what do we do? We have only three choices; go back, stop in place, or forge ahead.

What is she talking about, you may be thinking. Get to the point already! I want to share my story with you. This is my journey on the road to finding my passion.

I am a proud member of Toastmasters International, a worldwide organization with nearly a quarter of a million members. Toastmasters is best known for being a speaking organization, but hold on there − it's so much more! It's about confidence. It's about setting and achieving goals. Most importantly, it's about excellence in all you do. I stumbled upon this organization purely by accident on the road to finding my passion.

Trying to carve out a niche in the workplace, I was stumped. I was searching for learning opportunities, but company funds were not plentiful and my employer was holding those purse strings shut with a vice grip. I wasn't sure how I would set myself apart. At the behest of a co-worker, I agreed to check out a Toastmasters meeting. I wasn't enthusiastic about it, but went with the goal of simply becoming a better speaker. I'm a talker and will command a microphone to speak or sing anytime, anyplace, if given half the chance. I figured I didn't need Toastmasters, but reluctantly walked through the doors of a club meeting.

That was less than two years ago.

What resulted was a journey down a road that continues to take me places I've never dreamed of. It's the road to finding my passion. I thought this would be a short road, a short journey that would end quickly.

I was wrong. The morning of my first speech, I was hooked. Much like a child who wants more candy, or an addict who must feed his or her addiction, I could not get enough. I wanted control of that lectern on an ever-increasing basis and could not get enough inside of my little club's walls. I began talking to those who were more experienced than I and the potential opportunities exploded! "What? I can visit and be a guest speaker in other clubs?" "I can even JOIN other clubs?" Wow. For this speaking junky, that was music to my ears, and so began the journey to chasing and finding my passion, a journey I travel to this day.

The end of the road? Absolutely not! The first year was full of learning opportunities in the world of public speaking. The second year I discovered a whole new world of leadership opportunities, and I was off to the races, like a kid in a candy store with a twenty in his pocket. More, more more! Gimmee, gimmee! Club officer, club president, assistant area governor and currently heading toward an area governor appointment for next year. I am a club coach who will have successfully revived a club by the end of this year. My fingers are in a lot of cookie jars, and I love it. Sales, Marketing, PR... Oh my! I'm currently working toward the highest distinction the organization awards; Distinguished Toastmaster, and I am about halfway there.

It's not always been a smooth, paved road, this journey to finding my passion. I hit a few large obstacles this past year and was sidelined with personal and professional challenges that pulled me out of my Toastmasters involvement. But what has my passion for Toastmasters done for me? It helped to pull me back in. The incredible people that I've met now seem like family, and I have all the support, love and encouragement a person could ever want as a result. Those obstacles in the road? My family, my friends and yes, my passion, are helping me to find a way around them, through them or over them. Yes, I am finding my passion, but the journey won't end anytime soon.

What happens when I achieve the ultimate goal of Distinguished Toastmaster? I haven't decided, because this road, this journey, can get bumpy sometimes, and goals must be adjusted accordingly. There are many forks in the road and decisions must be made as to which way I will go. But I am certainly not turning around and I'm not stopping for more than the occasional rest. That means whatever the future holds, I'm moving forward.

I find it interesting that I once thought finding my passion was a destination, but I now see this is not the case. The passion is found in the journey. As we move down the road, there is so much to do, see and learn. If you are moving down the right road, you have found your passion, and the destination no longer seems as important.

If you haven't guessed by now, my passion is public speaking and leadership within the Toastmasters International organization.

When you find your passion and are moving down the right road, you will find joy and fulfillment beyond anything you've envisioned. The work is hard but the rewards are great. You will likely find that this new passion will translate to other areas of your life. For example, what you learn about your passion for your family can carry over to your work life. Similarly, what I've learned from Toastmasters has made me far more focused and goal-oriented in my professional life. Find your passion and you will find yourself making goals and reaching for the stars in more than one area of your life. You will feel fulfilled. You will feel a sense of accomplishment that cannot be bought. It must be earned by stepping out and taking the journey.

I must warn you that on this journey to finding your passion, you may sometimes surprise yourself with what you can accomplish. How easily we underestimate ourselves at times. It is easy to determine if someone is passionate about something or someone. Their eyes light up and a smile is usually on their face. They are an expert on that someone or something and love to tell others about it. The next time you speak to someone who has found their passion, you will immediately know they are on one incredible journey.

About the author:

Linda Eenigenburg remains an active Toastmaster, having recently served as Area and Division Governor in her District. She also earned the title of Distinguished Toastmaster in 2011. She is currently a Metrics Analyst with Aon Hewitt and continues exploring all the exciting twists and turns this life has to offer.

My Story

By Dick Hattan

A colleague of mine approached me at the office one morning to tell me that her twenty-two year old son had been recently diagnosed with a malignant brain tumor and that she would need time off to visit him in California and prepare for the inevitable. Her stoic reaction and business-like demeanor shocked me but I readily agreed to do whatever I could to provide direction for her staff and keep her remotely involved in her work while she visited with her son.

Later in the morning I attended a communion liturgy at the Episcopal Church across the street from the hospital where I worked. At the communion portion of the liturgy, the priest offered to provide healing prayer and anointing with oil for anyone who wanted healing in their life or on behalf of someone else. I approached the communion rail and asked for healing for my colleague's son. At the close of the service, I returned to work.

The following day, my colleague met me again in my office to tell me that her son had just received a report from his oncologist whom he had seen the previous day. The report showed that the tumor had begun to recede. I related to my friend about the healing service that I had attended and my request for prayer for her son. She was thrilled and couldn't thank me enough for what I had done.

Needless to say, I was overwhelmed and humbled by the news and wondered whether my request for healing was the reason for the reversal in the growth of the tumor. I continued to seek healing prayer and over time the malignant tumor disappeared and the young man resumed a normal life.

I thought about this episode of healing for the next 10 years mentioning it briefly to my spouse and some close friends who encouraged me to pursue this apparent gift. One day an opportunity arose for me to speak with a retired Episcopal priest who himself was a gifted healer. I told him my story about the miraculous healing at a distance. He listened and smiled and then told me a few of his own stories of healing. He told me that God was working through me and that he would like to work with me to initiate a healing ministry in our church. That day, four years ago, was the beginning of something that has continued to grow and provide a future career direction for me.

We began to talk about establishing a healing ministry in the church and discovered other people who were interested in this type of ministry who had also wondered whether they too were given a gift of healing. We chartered a chapter of the Order of St. Luke, the Physician, in our church and now have 10 people active in the lay ministry of healing. On the fourth Sunday of each month, healing prayer is offered at each of our three communion liturgies. The number of people who seek healing prayer has continued to grow and many healings have taken place. It has been a remarkable experience thus far.

Discovering this passion that has consumed me for the last four years has led me in a number of different directions that I hadn't anticipated. I decided to attend seminary and pursue a Master of Divinity Degree so that I could eventually become a health care chaplain. I feel called by God to be a healing minister to people in times of extreme vulnerability and loss.

As part of my course of studies, I served as a Chaplain Intern at Good Samaritan Hospital in Downers Grove, Illinois. This unit of Clinical Pastoral Education helped me to realize that I was a minister, a pastor, a priest to the patients and the families that I sat with in the Emergency Department in the middle of the night. I functioned as their chaplain as I consoled families at the death of their loved ones and I offered my presence to them when all I had to offer was myself.

The lessons I learned were of far greater value to me than the comfort and solace I provided to people in their time of need. What I learned was that I am being called to this ministry and all the deaths I attended and people I prayed with were leading me in this direction.

While this was going on, I became involved in the issue of the mental health needs of military veterans, especially those veterans returning from our recent conflicts in Iraq and Afghanistan. Since many people knew that I was an Army veteran of the Vietnam War, I was encouraged to volunteer as a member of the Lake-McHenry Veterans and Family Services Governing Council, an advisory panel that was overseeing a $3.5 million federal grant to provide mental health services to veterans and their family members. I didn't seek this appointment but people who I know and respect a great deal convinced me that my skills and presence were needed.

While attending the bimonthly meetings of this group, I became aware of a program called *The Veterans Writing Project*, a program designed to teach military veterans how to express their feelings and experiences in the military by writing. A colleague of mine, Mary Margaret Maule, designed the curriculum for a program in McHenry County and I joined her as a co-facilitator for the first group of veterans in the program. We received donations for books from a number of Rotary Clubs in the area and we began to meet and chronicle our stories. Our group, Veterans Voices, now numbers ten veterans spanning wartime periods from Korea to Afghanistan.

I see this venture as an expansion of the healing ministry that I feel called to engage. As a military veteran, I can provide a unique perspective and understanding of the issues that face soldiers returning from a war zone. It is this program coupled with my understanding of the issues veterans face when returning to civilian life that are leading me to consider a second career as a chaplain and perhaps as a chaplain in the Veterans Administration where I can work with veterans on a daily basis.

As my present career in health care administration begins to wind down, I am looking forward with eager exuberance to the day when I can put on the nametag of Chaplain and minister to the needs of veterans and their families. The vocation or calling to become involved in the ministry or service of healing is something that began 40 years ago when I enrolled at Northwestern University in the Master of Management Program in Health Care Management. My career in health care administration has led me to grow closer to the people in need of health care and now with my plan to become a chaplain, I will begin to minister to them up close and personal.

About the author:

Dick Hattan has spent his entire working career in the health care industry in senior management positions in hospitals and retirement communities. He resides in Geneva, Illinois, with his wife, Karen and their dog Xoe. He is the author of *Healing Memories* http://www.amazon.com/Healing-Memories-Dick-Hattan/dp/1453532838, a book of poetry.

Realizing Your Passion - It's Your Career!

By Mark Cummuta

I was recently asked at a conference I was speaking at, "You are so obviously passionate about what you do! So how did you find your passion?" Similarly, I've been complimented by interviewers, clients, and my employers that my passion for my work is "refreshing." But have you ever thought about what "passion" is in this context, and why it's so important today? This is a discussion on the importance of passion, especially for those in a job search, how you can find your passion, and how I found my passion, as well.

We all know people who are so absolutely passionate about what they do that their enthusiasm is infectious. But, why is being passionate about something related to your career critical? Short answer – because employers want passionate employees, because we have learned that all jobs are now temporary, and because no one should go through life doing something they don't love (or at least enjoy).

First, it is critical to be passionate in your career (and your job search if you are in transition) because employers want passionate employees, and teams want members who are passionate and excited by the project. "People want to be around positive, engaging people who might make you laugh, have the guts to ask questions and the guts to demonstrate that they are aware of your world. And, most certainly, people want to hire people who are eager to work hard, embrace each and every opportunity and moment...." (Molly Fletcher) < http://www.mollyfletcher.com>.

As illogical as this next point seems, especially since recruiters, human resources (HR), and even most hiring managers first look to EXCLUDE candidates if they don't have all the experience criteria they have added to a position's requirements, "...in the final analysis an employer would rather have someone on his/her team who was passionate than someone who had all the required experience." (Paul Megan) <http://www.streetdirectory.com/travel_guide/20968/careers_an d_job_hunting/job_seeking_passion____ignore_it_at_your_peril.h tml>

Continuing on, Paul Megan says, "Employers have much higher expectations.... they're only interested in candidates who show job seeking passion. And this is shown by taking the time to learn something about the organization and the hiring decision-maker--specifically their goals and passions. The candidate with job seeking passion will come forward with ideas about how he/she can make a difference to the organization and contribute to the passion of the employer."

The second reason finding your passion is critical to your career is because we have all learned now that every job is temporary. I know individuals that were absolutely critical to a firm's bottom-line, and yet were laid off. At my brother-in-law's firm, they had to lay off 20- and 30-year veterans, employees with in-depth corporate knowledge of the equipment and processes the firm relied on, in order to keep the company lucrative. You can still get laid off from a job that you are passionate about, but that does not mean your passion will be snuffed out. Jobs, and even companies, may come and go but if you are passionate about something you will find a way to get and stay involved. And as the saying goes, "Do the work that you love, and the money will follow."

And finally, we all deserve to do work in our career that we enjoy, if not outright love. We can no longer depend on our employers to find meaningful tasks and exciting opportunities for us. Rather, it is up to each of us to find where our passion lies, and then actively pursue opportunities that will pay us for what we love to do. (Meg Guiseppi) <http://executiveresumebranding.com/work-your-passion-fit-your-career-with-your-personal-brand/>.

Finding Your Career Passion

So let's talk about your career passion for a moment. Again, I can almost hear several readers asking, "But how can you be passionate about … 'work'?"

Jason Monastra of LambentPath is another author who has written about defining career passion, and his research has found that "A person is said to have a passion for something when they have a strong positive affinity for it. A love for something and a passion for something are very similar feelings."

Personally, I love the quote from Albert Einstein, one of my childhood heroes. Einstein once said, "Actually, I have no special talents. I am only passionately curious." Considering what Einstein accomplished, starting from a clerk's job in the US Patent Office, it's clear that his passion pushed him to the edge and beyond in his pursuit of knowledge. It is Einstein's kind of passion, that wake-up-and-want-to-go-at-it passion, that this-is-a-challenge-that-I-really-want-to-solve passion, that "I can see it in your eyes" passion that employers and clients look for … albeit perhaps without Einstein's penchant to wear the same clothes every day of the week.

One of the ways you can tell you're passionate about something is because you are not only open to learning more about it, and in fact actively look for all opportunities to do so, but you also drop your natural self-consciousness and will ask others for their advice on the subject.

Another way you can tell if you are passionate about something is the effort you put into it. When I think about the effort and results of someone who is passionate about what they do, the example I immediately think of are doctors; would you rather your doctor be in the top 10% of their class or the bottom third? Passion drives effort, which begets excellence!

Yet another way you can tell you are passionate about something is how it is very frequently on your mind, even intruding on other aspects of your life and your time! The easiest example of this is when you first realize you are personally in love – you can't help but think about that person, and you look for ways to be spend time with him or her.

A less intense example might be your favorite hobby or pastime. Everyone has something they do that they look forward to – your eyes light up, you smile, and there is no procrastination in doing that something every chance you get. For me, it's reading. I devour books (when I have time), sometimes two or more in a day. While my favorite genre is science fiction, I have always enjoyed reading across subjects, as well, and frequently pick up books, magazines, and articles from hard science to cooking, and from architecture to psychology, just because I love to read and learn.

Finally, a fun way to help point the way to what your passions may be would be to find a copy of your résumé that you are most proud of – it needs to be a few pages long for this to work best – or if you keep a blog, that would work even better. Import it into the online tool, Wordle <http://www.wordle.net/>, which creates a "cloud tag"-like visual representation of the words used. Those words that you use most frequently may just be related to your passions.

So let me explain how I found my passion, and hopefully that will help you think about yours, as well.

How I Found My Career Passion

I am passionate about many things - my wife, our kids, the U.S. Marine Corps, the defense of our country's hard-won freedoms, and lazy Saturday mornings watching cartoons or the ocean waves with my family, to name a few. But I also love several things about my career. Specifically, I am passionate about building and improving systems, processes, and people.

For many years now I've been a subject matter expert (SME) on data warehousing (DW), CRM (customer relationship management), and BI (business intelligence) systems. I've developed and integrated these applications around the world for over twenty-five years, written about them, and spoken at conferences about their best practice solutions. Many people through the years have commented about my apparent passion for these systems.

However, I realized several years ago that while an SME of these systems, my real passion was not WHAT these systems are. Rather, my passion is for WHO and WHY these systems are. CRM and BI applications and their accompanying DWs exist to help businesses improve what they do for their customers. As a customer, I am impressed with firms who can help me with my questions no matter how I communicate with them and who are able to offer me products and services that seem customized for me. That has translated into my excitement for providing the systems necessary to connect with and care for customers.

Once I realized this, I looked even closer, and I saw that developing and improving applications, and the people and processes that deliver these to the business is something that has been my driving passion throughout my entire career.

For example, my first year as a programmer I created a conversion program on my own time that helped me eliminate our last remaining library of very old legacy source code. [It also eliminated the need for my maintenance of that prior code, which I despised to maintain, so that I could move on to better projects ... as they say, necessity is the mother of all inventions!]

Similarly, when I learned client, project, and applications development methodologies, I developed numerous improvements for these. After I had tested them, I then mentored others in building, managing, and leading, which led to significant improvements in internal and external customer satisfaction.

My managers and mentors through the years have encouraged my passion, as well. This has allowed me to be certified in and utilize many of the leading process improvement methodologies – IT Service Management (ITSM), IT Infrastructure Library (ITIL

2011), Six Sigma, Lean Six Sigma (LSS), Design For Six Sigma (DFSS), Kaizen, Kanban, Total Quality Management (TQM), Business Process Improvement (BPI/BPM/BPR), Change Acceleration Process (CAP), and several others. I've then used what I've learned and applied through experience in mentoring numerous teams and projects.

Now I have to admit that I've been lucky. I was able to grow in my career, moving from technology that excited me, to exploring and finally realizing my passion!

Recently, as a Board Member for Hiring for Hope, the CIO for JobAngels, and as a speaker for both process improvement and for job search skills (e.g., Marine for Life <www.MarineforLife.org>, TechExecs <www.techexecs.net>, CIO Magazine's "CIO Job Search: A Real Life Chronicle" <http://advice.cio.com/blogs/cio_job_search_a_real_life_chronic le>, I've been able to train and mentor thousands of people on finding their passion. It's not always easy, and for some people it is an uncomfortable process to work through to find their career passion, but it is always exciting when you finally do realize your passion! And more so if you can then find work in the area that you're passionate about!

So, what are you waiting for? What are you passionate about? What makes your eyes light up and has you want to jump up and find time to do it now? And of course, now that you are starting to get excited about your passion, what are you going to do about it?!

The funny thing about finding and following your passion – sometimes you don't know where it will take you! Ask Colonel Ray J. Garcia (Retired); he fell in love with math and science in high school, and it landed him in the US Air Force's Space Program <http://www.usaa.com/inet/ent_blogs/Blogs?action=blogpost&b logkey=newsroom&postkey=2012_usaa_90th_anniversary>!

And with that, I need to put some more serious thought into finding ways to combine my passions for building and improving systems, processes and people, and watching the waves from the beach with my beautiful bride of twenty-five years!

Start Now! How You Can Find Your Passion!

Time is ticking. If you are waiting, there is no better time than today to find your passion. Don't wait for tomorrow. You cannot take back a day lost. Find your passion and start living your fullest life today.

You can turn your dreams into reality.

Determine what your passion is. Set your sights on your goal and be tenacious!

About the author:

Mark Cummuta, strategic executive consultant to the US Department of Defense and Board member for Hiring for Hope <http://www.hiringforhope.org/board-of-directors.html>.

Mark, as CIO/CTO & VP with full P&L authority, led award-winning product development, consulting services teams and his own CIO Advisory Services firm since 2003. A speaker and author on CIO & startup strategies, ITSM/ITIL and BPM, Lean Six Sigma, data warehousing and executive search he served our country as a US Marine. Mark earned dual MBAs from Loyola University of Chicago, studied Intellectual Property Protection law and is named on several technical patents.

Find Your Passion, Find Your Life

By Matt Lossau

> "To be alive is a fine thing. It is the finest
> thing in the world, though hazardous. It is a
> unique thing. It happens only once in a
> lifetime. To be alive, to know consciously
> that you are alive, and to relish that
> knowledge - this is a kind of magic. Or it
> may be a kind of madness, exhilarating but
> harmless." - Edna Ferber

Life--your DNA, your life experiences, your skills and giftings, your faith--has left its thumbprint on your life. This thumbprint defines your passion. It is unique to you, and fills a need the world has in a way no one else can.

Even more than your passion, life's thumbprint defines your mission. Passion evokes feelings of excitement and energy; mission carries those same feelings, and adds the dimension of purpose. Think of the times in your life when you have felt most fully alive. There is a thread, common to those experiences, which gives a clue to what your mission is. And when you are living out your life's mission, there is no feeling on the planet that compares--it is truly living.

Why are you here? We all want to feel useful--it is a basic human need. When you have identified your mission, it shapes the day-to-day decisions you make in life.

There is a longing, deep down inside of me, to do something that matters--really matters. My soul craves work that is meaningful and has a purpose and that I am good at. However, I have been woefully incompetent at consistently finding such meaningful work.

I have spent a lot of time--most of my adult life, if I'm truly honest--in a state of discontent. I am tempted to call it wasted time, but that isn't quite accurate. Much of the time I have floundered in discontent has turned out to be an investment--it has been the fuel that pushes me forward, refusing to be satisfied with a life of compromise.

My desire has been to find my passion--my life's mission--and begin to live from it. I have carried a romantic notion in my head of one day having an epiphany that would make everything clear. From that day forward, I would live a life of passion and purpose, and life would be filled with excitement and fulfillment.

I slowly--very slowly--began to realize that finding my passion is hard work and is very much a process. It does not reveal itself accidentally and it rarely comes suddenly. As my romantic ideal gave way to reality, I made two discoveries. The first is that we already have our passion; even if we don't readily know what it is, the passion is right there under the surface and will become clearer as we move toward it. The second--and perhaps more important--discovery, is that finding our passion is much more about action than analysis.

I found my passion, and ultimately my life's mission, thanks to the challenge of a friend. He challenged me to take action and create a project that would call out the best in me. He invited me to take a look around my world and see where my heart cried out to make a difference; what were the things I had been tolerating, or thinking that I couldn't--our shouldn't--take on? The beauty of this challenge is that it was a single project--not a lifelong commitment. The duration of the project could be as long or short as I liked. I suddenly had permission to take action, and move toward my mission. It was one of the greatest gifts I have ever been given.

Immediately upon hearing this challenge, I knew I wanted to do something to address extreme poverty. However, I began to feel like this was a once in a lifetime opportunity, and I was feeling the pressure to choose the absolute perfect project, in order to not squander the opportunity. I am so grateful I was able to see where that path was leading--a never-ending road of uncertainty, doubt, and inaction. Thankfully I decided to move forward with doing something to address poverty. The decision to take action and move forward is the key; you cannot live your passion--or even find it--if you do not take action. The key is to just go with your initial response, and take action. If nothing jumps out, make your best guess and start moving. There is a saying that you can't turn a parked car. Get moving and change course if you make new discoveries along the way.

I decided I was going to raise enough money to dig a deep well in a village in Kenya, to provide clean drinking water for an entire village. I jumped in and began researching organizations I could partner with and began talking to people about it. I didn't have a plan yet, but I began telling people I was digging a well, anticipating I would get more clarity as I went along. Telling people I was doing this was scary for me and it felt risky. My insecurities told me "people are going to think you're crazy, or have an over-inflated ego. Being able to say I was doing this as part of a project took some (not all) of that fear away, because it didn't feel like I was off chasing windmills, but was doing this because it was part of a project.

As I began to educate myself about deep wells, I found more clarity. I decided I wanted to do something more holistic than just digging a well. I continued to research and talk to people, and a plan began to develop.

I decided I wanted to adopt a village, by partnering with Global Hope Network International (GHNI). GHNI has a program that allows business, civic groups and other organizations, to sign up for a 3-year commitment to adopt an extremely poor village, to raise money and partner with them in achieving sustainability in the areas of food, water, wellness, income, and education. There were five other families in our neighborhood who I knew to be filled with compassion, and willing to take action, and

I asked them to join my family in adopting a village--and they agreed!

We just completed our 3-year partnership with the village of Gambella, in northern Kenya. Since we started our partnership with them, the village has been completely transformed. Where a handful of children used to meet under a tree, whenever a teacher happened to be in the village, there now stands seven classroom buildings, with eight full-time teachers, and their school has won awards from the Kenyan government for most-improved school in the area.

They have water for drinking and will soon have a windmill to provide very cheap water for irrigating their crops, which they learned how to plant and harvest for food as well as for income. They have a new wellness center and access to medical assistance without having to walk 15km to the nearest town. The people of Gambella have formed committees to sustainably manage their food, water, wellness, income, and education. They are learning how to affordably create their own personal greenhouses. The poorest among them now have homes, and others have seen how to easily build homes of their own, that keep the rain out.

They have friends on the other side of the world whom they have met (several of us--myself included--have been to visit them and work with them) and whom they know and love. Most importantly, they have hope for their future.

Where do you want to make a difference? What is the longing in your heart--the "what if" that keeps coming to mind for you? What is the hope and longing in your heart that you are afraid to acknowledge? That's where your passion is. It can be scary to explore your passion. Your passion is where your heart is, and fear of a broken heart has prevented many people from experiencing life, excitement, and freedom. There is risk in pursuing your passion, but the cost of avoiding that risk is enormous.

Perhaps you are like me, and you need to be given permission--
or a challenge--to explore your passion. If so, allow me to challenge
you. I challenge you to feel the tug in your heart; the tug you have
been ignoring and suppressing. Let the tug turn into an all-out pull;
imagine what it could become if you pursued it with reckless
abandon.

If you don't know what your tug is, stop what you are doing,
and look around your world. What is it that upsets you, or excites
you? Identify that thing, and go for it. Pick a project around that
passion, and move forward with it. Don't worry about having it all
planned out. Allow yourself to be fuzzy--very fuzzy--about what it
looks like, and just move forward. Do not worry about creating a
project that changes the world--the mere action of moving forward
with your half-baked plan will change the world. This isn't
something that needs to define the rest of your life--it's just a single
project. If it flops, so what? It's just a single project.

I also encourage you to invite others into your project. Let it be
known what your intentions are for the project, and watch as your
energy spreads and amplifies. You could keep it to yourself, and
still experience some of the benefits of exploring your passion, but
you would be robbing the rest of us. We need what you have to
offer.

As your project takes shape, and your purpose sharpens, spend
time analyzing it, and putting words to it. Describe your passion,
and try to put it in the framework of a mission--excitement and
adventure, combined with purpose. Choose your words carefully.
Make them succinct. You will be crafting your life mission, which
can be used to filter all of your life's decisions through. Not sure if
you should take that promotion, or agree to the volunteer position
you've been asked to fill? Run it through your mission and see if it
is a fit.

As I have gone through my project with Gambella, I have
revisited my own mission statement numerous times, revising it--
sometimes even starting from scratch. My current version is that "I

lead and challenge ordinary people, to take audacious actions that bring hope to the hopeless." While the words have changed somewhat over the past few years, the passion behind it has remained consistent, and has been gaining sharper focus. I feel most alive when my actions are aligned with this mission.

Finding your passion and life mission can be a scary and difficult thing. It is also one of the most exciting, rewarding, and world-changing endeavors you ever undertake. When living out of your passion, your energies multiply, and the results are amazing. If you find yourself stuck in identifying your passion, I encourage you to seek out a life coach, to help you through the process. You can also take a look at my blog, which has some ideas to help start you thinking through the process (http://justiceandlife.org/how-to-perform-a-brain-reset/).

Go ahead, you have my permission to make a difference in your world--it could be one of the greatest gifts you ever give for yourself!

I would love to hear from you if you start a project of your own—drop me a line at matt@mattlossau.com.

About the author:

Matt Lossau is just an ordinary guy, with an ordinary job, and a belief that the world is best changed by ordinary people. He is passionate about leading and challenging ordinary people to take audacious actions that bring hope to the hopeless. Follow him at http://mattlossau.com, http://justiceandlife.org/ and on Twitter @MattLossau.

Roaring Passions

By Stefan Levy

I saw my entire body reflected in the eye of Chaucer, a serious male lion, whose 3-inch canines were quite visible as he accepted a chicken leg offering with a low rumble.

I knew then that my feeling about and relationship with the Top Cats of the jungle would never be the same. While he engulfed the chicken leg, he also engulfed my entire being into his all knowing eyes and I felt privileged to be in his majestic presence. He was the one giving me the gift of sharing his space on this planet with me. He rumbled some tones to let me know there was power behind those pipes, should he desire to display it. He devoured the chicken leg with thanks in a few snaps and then looked directly at me, powerfully directing me to provide another, lest his rumbles crank up considerably. As I quickly complied and as he quickly dispatched the next "potato chip", he made it clear, and I felt compelled to speak to him, saying, "I know. You're the Lion. Just because there is this fence between us, I'm not forgetting that fact".

Being in his presence humbled me. Chaucer and 75 other lions, tigers, bears, (oh my) all live at the Valley of the Kings Sanctuary (VOTK), located just past the Illinois border in Sharon, Wisconsin. It is a sanctuary, home, final destination for abused and abandoned animals like Chaucer.

Very interesting: The lions roar a greeting to Harleys! Only to Harleys. Seems the vibration of the Harley Davidson engine is the right pitch and they think it is another big cat! Well, when we all arrived, they were certainly correct in greeting other "Top Cats"! This particular ride was sponsored by the Top Cats Motorcycle Club, a generous group of north suburban business people who also love motorcycles, another Passion Poster Child, certainly one of mine.

A number of people have approached me after the ride to excitedly offer some support. Please, keep the support in motion after the initial excitement has worn off. These animals need us and our help!

As I got to know the cats by name and history, they would come to the fence and greet me. Tigers "chuff" a greeting. What an experience to look at that thin (but strong) fence and have a 1000 pound, 10 ft long tiger come over, press against the fence and "chuff" a friendly hello greeting and want a treat. I tell you what, my earlier respect for them as fearsome predators, has been elevated to another level. They are awesome creatures, more so when you get to know them on a personal level. What an opportunity! To become acquainted with them on a personal level! Whew!

During the ride a transformation went kind of like this: Wow, we're going to take a really cool ride and get to interact with some big cats up close and personal, like no place else. Let's get a good route; pray for good weather and then Let's Roll! Upon meeting the volunteers and clearly seeing their dedication, passion and commitment I began to wonder about that. Why do they come up there every weekend, some from great distances, to lend a hand? Once I met the animals and heard all the stories about their plight, I got infused with some of that passion. Other visitors have caught the same passion. The ride became about more than a cool ride to a neat place. It also became about how we could help these animals of the jungle, now in man's care.

There clearly became some spiritual, cosmic aspect to all this. Bikers often wear clothing and paint their bikes with images of animals. Why? Their beauty? Power? Freedom? Symbolism? American Indians did the same thing. Bikers are often compared to Indians on steel ponies. This was an opportunity to connect with those animals on another level, not ever experienced by most of the people on the planet. Whenever I pull in there I crank my bike, then shut it off. The lions respectfully wait till I am done "roaring".

Then they set off a chorus that just has me standing there, eyes closed, drinking in their primeval call, which resounds throughout my entire being. One of the very artistically talented volunteers, Chris, made a CD called *Togar's* (a beautiful stately male lion who has since passed) *Dream* with lots of cats roaring. I now start my day with this! Putting a tiger in my tank (even though tigers chuff and lions roar - you get the idea). These CD's are for sale at the Sanctuary.

The stories were truly heartbreaking about what people have done to these animals. Charlie, the black panther, can only eat ground meat because a Hollywood producer had his teeth and claws removed. Nook, the huge 1300 pound Liger (half lion half tiger) was bred for his coat to be on someone's wall. Penny, the cougar was toted around by a trucker in his cab. Koke Joe, a beautiful tiger was a circus performer till he got too old and they were going to put him down. Others were to be used in canned "hunts" where they chain the cat to a post and some big gun "hunter" shoots it. Hearing about that flamed passions of another sort, like a protective mother bear. This place is truly a sanctuary, an orphanage and rest place for these majestic animals. They are alive only because they are here and people support this place.

It gives me great pride to say that Top Cats of Illinois motorcycle club was very giving and supportive to the sanctuary. We raised $2200 for the animals that day. Some of our group has joined as supporters. Others are considering it. I hope you choose to join and support them. They told me that they had a little concern before we came - about a group our size. About us following rules; being safe; keeping the animals safe. After we left, they said that we were an orderly, under control, easy to work with group of caring, responsible adults welcome back any time! What a compliment! That our style of safe, orderly fun riding translated over so apparent in our behavior there.

VOTK (http://www.votk.org) exists only on donations - most in the form of "membership" which entitles one to visit the sanctuary and bring friends. I encourage everyone to "join". Sponsorship of an animal costs $250 per month, to feed that animal the whole year. I encourage you to consider this.

Each one who was there, I am sure has stories and photos to share. The excitement of sharing space and a meal with such awesome predators, who were friendly and happy to get our treats, prevailed throughout the day. Everyone went home with a new experience under their belt. Donations flowed. Everyone was so very generous. I wish to personally thank everyone who unflinchingly donated and will in the future donate food, money and support.

Jim and Jill (who operate VOTK) blessed me with quite a gift, which I honor greatly: Sometimes lions shed some mane. They gave me a little piece of mane. In lion country the mane stands for strength and protection. Currently I have this wrapped around a lion statue next to pictures of my kids. I suspect it will make its way somehow to my bike! I have brought my kids and friends to visit the animals. They loved the experience.

All in all, the Big Cats ride was very successful from my point of view; safe; great weather; exciting; great camaraderie; new experiences; and a chance to give back something to these beautiful animals who simply seek to survive conditions humans have put them in. We'll do this again next year! We hope you can join us!

Keep the rubber down!

About the author:

Stefen Levy, (steflink@ameritech.net) President Management Search, enjoys multiple passions at the same time. His has unbridled love and respect for big cats, motorcycles and blues www.cruisinblues.com on his Harley iPod. He led 100 bikes from the Top Cats Motorcycle Club www.topcats.org to visit and support some magnificent lions, tigers and bears, oh my!

A Passion for Passion

By Maria Odiamar Racho

For me, passion is feeling the fire and energy of life. It's about living and experiencing each moment to the absolute fullest. During times when I lack passion in what I'm doing, I feel like I'm just going through motions, numb and indifferent to what's around me. It is in having passion for what I am doing and in my whole being that the joy of life comes alive.

I have always been fascinated by others that have great intensity and at the same time peace in what they do. They are focused and there's an internal energy that radiates from them, whether it is the mechanic that talks about all of the possibilities of trouble shooting the problem with my car, or the professional athlete who's drive and ease draws you in to their experience, or the teacher inspiring and unleashing the potential in children. Others feel the energy passion gives off and it draws them in like a magnet. My passion has always been to find that in others and when possible help people find that in themselves. So, when asked to write this entry, I couldn't resist.

The work I do today has been the most fulfilling work I have ever done. So much so that it has bled into all aspects of my life by helping me become a more whole and alive being. I am an organizational effectiveness consultant for Allstate Insurance. We are on a journey of transforming our organization through individual transformations. What I have witnessed and have been blessed to be a part of has been the unleashing of our people in the organization. It is about tapping into and allowing our people to see the potential they have within them, which brings me back to how I have been able to find my own passion.

I have not been in this field for very long, just about two and a half years. Before this role, I was a manager progressing pretty well in my career to broader and greater responsibilities. As time passed, I found myself feeling stuck and like a robot, unaware that I was trying to pick up my energy by adding more work to my plate trying to address issues of low morale and disengagement in our department. During my last assignment, I had five managers reporting to me on three different continents. Each of those managers had about 12-15 employees. I would set up one on ones with their people to get to know them and talk to them about what they enjoy most about their work, what their strengths are, etc.

A co-worker of mine, who has always been a strong supporter and coach for me, noticed that something didn't seem right. She said that I didn't seem as engaged as she's used to me being. She sat me down and just seemed really curious about how I was. I didn't feel judgment from her, just curiosity and caring. As we began to talk, I realized that there were days that I left work feeling fulfilled and with high energy, then there were other days that seemed to just drain my energy. The latter seemed to be more and more frequent lately. She suggested I create two lists one to write down what I liked about my work and the other to write down what I didn't like. She also encouraged me to focus on my energy and note when my energy was high or low.

During the next couple weeks, I did just that, and I began to see a pattern. The days when I would spend time in one-on-one conversations with my employees, I would lose track of time and get totally consumed in hearing their stories, hearing their ideas for ways to improve their work, and focusing on their development. I also found high energy when I would go home and as a "hobby" I would research topics like culture change and leadership. The days that were focused on project issues, capacity forecasting and planning, writing statements of work, and so on were long and draining.

As I started to become aware of the work that I enjoyed the most, I began to look in other parts of the organization and to my amazement this position I have now was listed. I could not believe that I would be able to focus on building individual and organizational capabilities every day, all day and it would be considered work (no longer just a hobby). Let me be clear, I feel extremely blessed for this opportunity, but it has not been easy. These past couple years have been both the most challenging and most rewarding times of my career. Think about a hobby or sport you love, some of it may come naturally, but in order to develop, you need to push yourself sometimes beyond imagine in order to stretch.

I have found my passion through investing time in me, taking the time to learn about my strengths and embracing the differences that make me me. The more I learn and understand about who I am, the more I appreciate myself and everything around me.

Passion is about unleashing the gifts within us. I believe that we are perfect as we are, as God intended us to be, it's a matter of being aware that everything we need to live our fullest life comes from within and is influenced by the choices we make.

About the author:

Maria Odiamar Racho is an Organizational Effectiveness Consultant at Allstate Insurance. She studies culture change and leadership as her hobby while actively involved in various community efforts both in and out of work. Maria lives in Glenview, Illinois, with her husband and two children. She would love to hear what you are passionate about. http://twitter.com/mracho.

How JobAngels (And You) Have Changed My Life

By Mark Stelzner

What is this JobAngels thing and how did it begin?

Rumor has it that my crackling cornflakes whispered an idea to me on the morning of January 29th. It was apparently hard to decipher over their milk-drowned voices, but eventually I could make out their message - "help people find jobs". Their whole-grained wisdom spread to the world and all were saved. (End scene) Wow. So inspirational!

The real story is this. I was eating breakfast and thinking about the economy. We were in the throws of a debilitating week of job loss   announcements <http://money.cnn.com/2009/02/06/news/economy/jobs_janu ary/index.htm> and things looked to be worsening in all sectors. I had been spending a bit of time on Twitter <http://www.twitter.com/stelzner> and had accumulated about 700 followers, a large percentage of whom are experts and professionals in the HR sector. So I wondered, what if each of those followers helped just one person find a job? Could we actually make a difference? Here's the original Tweet:

> "Was thinking that if each of us helped just 1
> person find a job, we could start making a
> dent in unemployment. You game?"

How does it Work?

Begin by choosing someone to assist. This can be a friend, a colleague, a neighbor or a complete stranger. Then, simply help them in any that you can.

What if I Need Help?

Follow @JobAngels on Twitter or send us a Twitter direct message or post a message with the #JobAngels hash tag

<http://www.wildapricot.com/blogs/newsblog/archive/2008/03/11/an-introduction-to-twitter-hashtags.aspx> and we will put the word out.

Where did the name come from?

The response was immediate and overwhelmingly positive. Within several minutes, the discussion evolved to the use of a hashtag to help those in need locate those willing to help on Twitter. But what to call it? A few ideas floated around and then I sent this message on a whim:

> "Wish we could come up with a site/plan to
> link all this positive energy to. How's
> #jobangels sound? :)"

And thus JobAngels was born. It was literally that simple. This was not rocket science and there was no divine intervention. It was one simple idea that somehow tapped into people's desire to stop being victims to a seemingly endless stream of angst, depression and relentless negativity. When faced with hundreds of thousands of job losses, it's easy to feel overwhelmed and helpless. But if the idea is for you to simply aid one person - a friend, a family member, a colleague or a complete stranger - that somehow not only seems possible, it seems probable.

How have people responded?

It has been four months since that original message, and in that time, a movement has begun. In this short period, over 18,000 JobAngels have already assembled across Twitter <https://twitter.com/jobangels>, LinkedIn <http://www.linkedin.com/groups?gid=1789016> and Facebook <http://www.facebook.com/group.php?gid=47105839914>.
Over 500,000 JobAngel messages have been sent across a myriad of online platforms. Angels have donated their time, their networks, their expertise and their hearts to this grassroots initiative (and we are just getting started).

This grass-roots movement of workers who want to help others find jobs, is ready and willing to assist you. The response was instantaneous and overwhelmingly positive, Stelzner said.

Within an hour we had the name JobAngels and a Twitter site. Within two hours we were on LinkedIn, and by three, we were on Facebook. Currently, over 10,000 Twitter followers get the word out today. Our LinkedIn Group has over 8,500 members.

Let me be clear about one thing. JobAngels is not my movement, but it has changed my life. I am blown away by everyday people deciding to step up and aid those in need of employment. This is a chance to truly impact someone's life and it is amazing to watch the goodwill grow at a time when it's tempting to thrust your head in the sand.

Please join us, if you haven't already. I'm humbled to be part of this initiative and look forward to hearing your stories of success in the weeks and months to come. Thanks to those of you who have joined thus far and remember, just one Angel can make a world of difference.

NOTE: Five "Guardian Angels" have gone well beyond the call of duty in helping JobAngels become a reality. A warm and heartfelt thanks to Mark Cummuta <http://www.linkedin.com/in/markcummuta>, Chris Connolly <http://www.twitter.com/ccconnolly>, Deirdre Honner <http://www.thehrmaven.com/>, Charee Klimek <http://www.linkedin.com/in/chareeklimek> and Chris Bailey. Our current and future success would not be possible without their generosity and commitment to this cause. I'd also like to thank Greg Grigoriou of VanPaul Design for creating the JobAngels logo on such short notice. Visit JobAngeles.org to learn more.

How You Can Help

It begins by picking just one person. Please remember that assistance can come in many forms. This can range from a sympathetic ear to offering real-world advice, resume reviews, networking connections and much more. Ultimately, we are all simply helping to put people back to work one individual at a time.

Sign Up for "Taking Flight"

JobAngels is pleased to introduce *Taking Flight*, a newsletter that will help keep you informed of the latest and greatest from the JobAngels family. Please remember that we take the privacy of our community members very seriously. Email newsletter@jobangels.org with any questions.

About the author:

Mark Stelzner, founder of Inflexion Advisors <http://www.inflexionadvisors.com/>, brings twenty years of experience to internal and external HR transformational initiatives for public and private sector clientele worldwide. Mark has brought over $3.5 billion worth of value to his clients and employers.

Mark founded JobAngels.org, a grassroots non-profit organization dedicated to helping individuals find gainful employment, which merged with Hiring for Hope <http://www.hiringforhope.org/job-angels.html>.

A Passion to Make a Difference/Life with Larry

By Susan Schuerr

I peered into the sad eyes of a 27 year old 6'4"man named Bob who was imprisoned in his wheelchair. He had a handsome ruddy complexion and a desire to communicate. It wasn't long before he told me his life story. Five years ago he was in a snowmobile accident that left him paralyzed from the waist down. A few years later, he lost his mother. I wanted to comfort him like I would my own son. My heart was heavy when he responded fatalistically, "It is what it is."

We discussed medical science and the progress they were making helping people like Bob, and we talked about God and his plan for his life. "You know what I miss the most," he said, "the adrenalin rushes. That's why I am here at Adaptive Adventures <http://adaptiveadventures.org/>. I was hoping to ski today, but the slots are filled." I put it on my calendar to be at Wilmot Ski Resort when Bob tried a sit ski for the first time.

Adaptive Adventures provides an opportunity for a handicapped person to downhill ski with an able bodied person. My husband and I love volunteering with them. As fate would have it, Larry, my husband, was Bob's teacher. The lesson took a good part of the day, but by the end it all clicked for Bob who triumphantly cruised down the hill solo all the way to the lodge with Larry and his good friend following in his tracks. He was ecstatic about his new accomplishment, and he certainly experienced an adrenalin rush. Bob now has a passion for skiing and other sports offered by Adaptive Adventures. He now has hope for a better and more fulfilled future.

The week before, Larry worked with a client named Ted who was a Lieutenant Colonel in the Air Force while Larry was merely an E5 in the Marines. This was quite a role reversal for both of them. Larry's method of teaching was to treat the Vets as though he was their gunnery sergeant. "Turn left," he would shout. "Make it a harder left turn. Get up and do it again." Ted, Larry's client, was a pilot in the Air Force. When he was discharged, he joined the reserves and started working for United Airlines. But during the Iraq war, the Air Force Reserves took him from his job and family to serve his country. Ted suffered an injury as a result of a cargo plane crash. Today, he walks hunched over with a cane as a result of being partially paralyzed. But he has a passion for skiing; his dream is to continue working with Adaptive Adventures so he can join his lovely wife and child on ski adventures in Colorado.

While Larry worked with Ted, I volunteered with Vince, the gentle bulldog. He was a guerrilla sniper in the 80's. He talked about his deployments in Grenada, El Salvador and Panama. He vividly recalled a rescue effort of nuns and priests in El Salvador. Sadly, they were all executed before his team of guerrillas arrived. Vince suffered trauma on his final deployment and currently has a rebuilt shoulder and hip. He also suffered a stroke that has limited his movement on the left side. My fellow instructor could understand Vince's condition; he also suffered a stroke on the same side.

As the only able-bodied skier, my job was to demonstrate how to ski down the hill and to help Vince stay steady. We took him up on the magic carpet and worked on getting him down the bunny hill, which looked like Mt. Everest to him. Vince did fall a couple of times and we wanted him to quit, but quitting was not in Vince's vocabulary.

Larry and I are honored to volunteer with Adaptive Adventures. Seeing real heroes overcome their unbelievable obstacles speaks volumes to us about how to live life with courage and passion.

For more information about Adaptive Adventures see http://www.adaptiveadventures.org and to read more of Sue's writings see http://www.lifewithlarry.org.

About the author:

Susan Schuerr, an educator and writer, lives in Fox River Grove with her husband, Larry. They have three grown children and five grandchildren. Sue taught English and Drama at Cary-Grove High School in IL. She recently published a story in an anthology entitled *Falling in Love with You.* See http://www.lifewithlarry.org.

Presidential Pastry

By Wally Amos

Thanks to my work with literacy, it has been my privilege to spend time in the company of both George and Barbara Bush. George, I have met over the course of fairly formal occasions-- awards ceremonies, State Dinners, official receptions at the White House, and the smaller parties that followed. Barbara and I have worked more closely together championing the cause of literacy in America.

Whatever you feel about their politics, they are remarkable people. In addition to their being truly extraordinary individuals, each in their own right, they are also an exceptionally close couple. Their marriage is a strong, loving partnership.

I have great respect for George and Barbara and cherish the memories I have from my times with them. They've provided me with several recipes I'd like to share with you. You can bet their personal pantries are well-stocked with top-notch ingredients!

Let me tell you a story about the kazoo and President Bush.

I received the National Literacy Honors Award, from the White House, along with Harold McGraw, a titan in business and a real community servant, and adult literacy students and tutors. Barbara and George Bush made the presentations.

It was a very prestigious evening with entertainment provided by Barbara Mandrell, Patrick Swayze, and Morgan Freeman. It was truly a special evening and I felt so honored to be sharing it with such an illustrious group!

This particular event was also the first time television cameras had ever been allowed inside the East Room of the White House: ABC was recording it to be aired later as a special for national broadcast. Gary Smith and Dwight Hemian, two of television's quality people were the producers and did a beautiful job of it. It was just a wonderful occasion. I received my award, and it was a very somber, very special moment for me.

After the telecast, everyone involved in the ceremony was invited up to the second floor--the living quarters of the White House--for a post-ceremony party. Well, somehow Christine and I managed to be the first couple to arrive up there. I don't know how it happened, but there we were on our own, so we began looking around--I mean, the White House is a museum! Literally! There's just such a tremendous sense of history to the place. It suddenly struck me then how the power of the office of President is just that--the power of the office: of the title, of all that that building represents. The man who bears the title is honored to possess it, but only temporarily. His job is to uphold and strengthen it to the best of his ability, and then move on, leaving it for the next incumbent.

I was marveling at that insight as Christine and I continued to admire the living history that surrounded us, when at that moment, around the corner came George and Barbara Bush! Well, the very first thing that came to me to do was to whip out my kazoo and play "Hail To The Chief." I think George was a little startled, he didn't seem to know quite what to do, but Barbara started doing a little dance--she has a great knack for adapting to almost any situation.

We all had a nice laugh about it. And you know, it was just another Wally Amos Moment--where Wally Amos believes in having fun, even with the President of the United States! See, if I'd let myself get all intimidated by the office he represented and squashed my impulse to salute him with my kazoo, we would have all missed out on a really neat memory and a chance to connect on a very human level.

RECIPE FOR PRESIDENTIAL PASTRY:

Start with a healthy dose of Awareness of What's Appropriate.

Add a strong cupful of Appreciation of time and place.

Then leaven the mixture with equal amounts of Empathy and Humor.

Use a dash of Good Judgment to determine how long to work the mix—if underdone, the result will be less than memorable. If overdone, tough and hard to swallow. When this recipe works, it is a delight to all who share a laugh over it.

COOK'S NOTE: The key here is a very light touch!

About the author:

Wally Amos, America's favorite cookie baker personally produces small batches of his original cookies not far from his Honolulu home. They are literally hand-made from scratch from the exact recipe he used in 1975 when he opened the world's first cookie store. Visit Wamos Cookies <http://wamoscookies.com/>.

Brand New Strings

By April M. Williams

My husband Noel developed an ear for perfect pitch through many years of guitar practice and listening to music. He cringes when he hears an off key note sung or when an instrument is played out of tune. One of his favorite sounds is the bright tones of a new set of guitar strings. They have a special sound that is full and brassier than old, dull strings. When I watch him restring his guitar, I can see his excitement, as he anticipates listening to the initial strum of their clear vibrations. His enthusiasm is contagious and I find myself looking forward to listening as he plays those satisfying first notes. For Noel, the brand new strings bring out his passion for music and playing the guitar.

I played piano as a child but never developed this type of passion for making music. The hammers stuck the strings as I operated the keyboard with the technical mastery of a heavy equipment operator. I played notes as they were written on the sheet music not from within the depths of my soul. For me, my passion is the intersection of people and technology. I am passionate about my calling and for me, starting work each day is like restringing the guitar and strumming those first few notes. I do what I love and take pleasure in the fulfillment I get out of helping others to find their passion. Just like Noel, my passion is observable by others.

It is not that I don't enjoy music - because I do. Cross country journeys became more bearable with the stereo cranked up as we traveled closer to our next stop on route to our final destination. These were the days before GPS receivers and we would depend upon our map folded up to show only the area just ahead of and behind us. We needed few resources on these trips. Besides the map, cassette tapes and a full tank of gas, we stocked up on snacks and a cooler full of pop.

My professional journey has taken several turns and has even been re-routed a number of times throughout the years. I worked in retail and small offices early in my professional life before moving into the world of Fortune 50 corporations. Experience in merchandising, technology, education, finance and ecommerce across multiple industries are segments of highway I passed through on my career path. I earned my Bachelor's and Master's degrees as a working mom with young children learning to focus on taking one step at a time to reach my destination. Insights from mentors guided me and helped me navigate unspoken corporate politics. It was all part of the trek my career was taking.

Several years ago I found myself at a crossroads in my own professional field. Consistent, dependable performance led to promotions and increased responsibility in the corporate world. I demonstrated a willingness and desire to learn through formal college education and self-training. As a technical project manager, I researched the criteria necessarily to earn certification as an industry recognized Project Management Professional (PMP). On nights and weekends I poured over the study material and passed the PMP certification test. Through seminars and internet research I stayed up to date with industry trends.

As I continued to move ahead in my profession, I found less satisfaction in my particular career. The people in my office mattered to me and I enjoyed projects where I could make a tangible improvement in a co-workers career. I continued to deliver results though I wondered if that was all there was to my line of business. It became a struggle to get excited about projects I worked on, as the thrill inside me was gone. I wondered if it was too much to ask for personal satisfaction with my employment as well as a paycheck?

I began my search for something more though I had no idea where the journey was going to take me. As it turned out, my route was not going to be a straight path between two points but more of a meandering adventure sampling a variety of opportunities along the way. The excursion itself was part of my own transformation and learning process. I discovered my true talents lied in what I could do to help others achieve their goals. I felt passion and most successful when I nurtured success in others.

My career evolution did not happen over a single voyage but rather through many small journeys. Over a few months time, I watched as my entire world changed. I lost my bearings as I found I was using a road map for the wrong state. Physical symptoms began to plague me and stress was making it hard to concentrate. Illness and other challenges within my family demanded my attention. The economy took a toll on the company I was employed by and I was let go. When I found myself unemployed, it finally brought my professional concerns front and center. I was forced out of my comfort zone as my expectations for myself and my anticipated career direction were knocked for a loop. I knew I could not return to the Fortune 50 world where I grew and developed my career but now I did not know which way I should turn.

It took a while for the right path to begin to unfurl as suggestions from others trickled in. Ideas and concepts percolated through my mind and I filtered and explored various strategies. Personal reflection, research and investigation began. The ideal course of action did not come into view as a sudden vision of inspiration. Rather than emerge as a complete roadmap, my destiny became visible segment by segment like the view along a winding road. As I traversed down the path and around the bend, I could now see as far as the next curve in the road. This itinerary included a few expeditions along detours and closed roads as well as few wrong turns that were also part of my journey.

Looking back through my career I thought about the times I felt the greatest satisfaction in my work. The most rewarding situations for me were where I leveraged technology and people to make a difference. I considered the activities I liked to do in my personal life and what gave me the most pleasure in my free time. I enjoyed building relationships with others, continuous learning and traveling. My internal compass for morals, ethics and values weighed in also. I had to be authentic in whatever I did. How could I take all the concepts, ideas, skills and knowledge that were important to me and leverage these into my next career?

Financial considerations weighed in too. I was making a good living at my corporate job with generous benefits. If I changed careers it was likely the starting salary would be considerably lower than I was earning. My family and I had become accustomed to a certain standard of living and my choices could impact not just me but them also. My pay scale could impact our future retirement plans as well.

Gradually, I found myself letting go of preconceived ideas and expectations for myself. As I did so, I was open to soak up new ideas from unexpected sources. People around me asked me to coach them on their personal marketing and professional brand development. Organizations courted me as a speaker to share my social media knowledge. There were calls for interviews as a subject matter expert on effective job search techniques. Career centers asked me to leverage my technology background to provide group training on social marketing tools. Little by little a new career began to reveal itself for me. By releasing myself from expectations I was open to the incoming flow from unexpected sources.

The journey has been well worth the trip and I have found renewed enthusiasm and excitement in my work. The sense of satisfaction is palpable in me. I feel excited and look forward to starting my workday early in the morning. I was taken aback as to how powerfully other people reacted to my zeal. What a feeling I have when I hear comments like these:

> "I can see how passionate your are about
> your work. Your excitement is contagious."

"You shine. You actually seemed to glow. When you talk about social marketing you light up."

"There is a physical transformation in you when you talk about helping others."

In my role as a marketer and coach, I talk with people every day who tell me they are unsatisfied by their career. They feel unfulfilled and an emptiness inside. There is a lack of direction, desire and purpose they are searching to find in their professional life. They long to make their mark and leave a positive impact on the world. They yearn to leave a legacy. I get questions like "Is that all there is to a career?" I can empathize because I found myself in the exact same crossroads before I transformed my career and my life.

About the author:

April M. Williams is passionate about increasing business revenue through social media marketing. April has guided learners of all levels, from the social media phobic to the experienced, on how to develop credibility and create their brand. A nationally recognized speaker, author and trainer, April shares her marketing tips via CyberLife Tutors <http://www.cyberlifetutors.com/>blog and books <http://amzn.to/Zgq6Nm>.

My Challenge to You

Thanks for reading our stories!

I'm sure you found the stories inspiring, valuable and energizing as I have. My co-authors encouraged me through their words and I am pleased to share these anthologies with you.

Now, it's your turn to ignite your passion and perhaps chart a new course for your life. It is only when you share your passion with others that will you feel the real power inside you. You owe it to yourself to find your focus in life that will bring you fulfillment and satisfaction.

Spark your internal flame. Get glowing. Start now. Don't wait even a moment! Begin your journey to find and follow your passion.

Would you like to share your personal account of finding, following or living your passion? Join the conversation online at http://www.cyberlifetutors.com/store/ignite-your-passion-book/. To share your account in Ignite Your Passion Volume 2, email April M. Williams april@cyberlifetutors.com.

Thanks again.

- April M. Williams

We Love Reviews!

Would you be willing to write a review http://amzn.to/Zgqo6T on Amazon.com so I know if you liked these stories or not? I would really appreciate it.

- April M. Williams

Other Works by April M. Williams

Social Networking Throughout Your Career
http://amzn.to/WirUX5

Networking For Results
http://www.cyberlifetutors.com/store/

Press Pause Moments http://amzn.to/YWy4ZC